Dr Joanne Orlando

Life Mode

On

How to feel less stressed, more present and back in control when using technology

Hardie Grant

BOOKS

Dr Joanne Orlando (PhD, M.Ed, B.Ed) has spent over fifteen years studying our relationship with technology and how to make it less stressful, happier and more fulfilling. She publishes cutting-edge research, and has developed terms such as 'sharenting' and 'zombie scrolling' which have now entered everyday lexicon. Dr Jo provides solutions to today's most pressing digital lifestyle issues through keynote presentations, articles, TV and podcasts worldwide, and is the creator of digital literacy education program TechClever. She lives in Sydney, Australia.

For Alana, Tom and Jack.
You mean the world to me.
I couldn't ask for a better
support team!

Contents

Introduction

Technology is supposed to make our life easier, but this isn't always the reality. All around the world, people are struggling with the amount of time, effort and headspace they lose to technology. Our reliance on technology is affecting family and career balance, interfering with personal life goals and interpersonal relationships, and causing issues with parenting and marriages.

We want technology in our lives – we would struggle to live without it – but it is making us feel stressed and exhausted. This book will change that for you.

I have spent close to two decades studying our digital life and working out how we can have a better relationship with technology. I have interviewed hundreds of people from all walks of life about their technology use (many of whose experiences you'll find in this book). I have studied and worked within university research centres, key multinational organisations and governments around the world. And in all that time, one finding has hit me hard: our technology use is causing personal and professional problems on a scale we've never seen before.

Maybe it's because we adopted technology later in life. Unlike the generations after us, today's adults have had a messy and unplanned transition into a digital lifestyle. Using our devices, apps and sites in ways that benefit our life is not coming naturally.

If used well, technology can extend our ability to think and problem-solve, and enhance our creativity. However, when it is not used well, it can cause chaos and damage that exacerbate the pressures and insecurities of our life, and have damaging impacts on our career, relationships and sense of worth.

Do you relate to any of these problems?

'I can't get my husband's attention anymore, he is always on Instagram.'

'I'm busy. Really busy. Technology is supposed to make life simpler, but it's the opposite. I don't have any time to myself.'

'I have tried to digital detox for the fifth time this year. I know that I use technology too much and it's not healthy for me. I really want to change.'

'I kept count while I was reading a book, and I actually reached for my phone 22 times in an hour.'

'I look at my screen more than anything else in the day, even more than I look at my girlfriend.'

'I find myself writing one more email in my bed, emailing from the toilet, emailing while I'm cooking dinner. I am supposed to be in control of technology, but technology is controlling me.'

'I find it difficult to focus on what I read online and to remember it. I have so much information swimming inside my head.'

'My teenage daughter is obsessed with her phone. I can't get her off it. We argue all the time about technology.'

'We don't have sex much anymore. Instead we're either watching Netflix or on our phones.'

These types of issues have emerged fairly recently, in the last five years. They have quickly become deep problems because they are not being resolved. Instead, they are eating away at our wellbeing and our quality of life.

Technology is no longer something that we simply use, it has become part of who we are. We have a relationship with it.

Technology is not going away. In fact, it's likely to become increasingly pervasive in the future. Think how much your technology use has changed in the last couple of years alone. How do you think we will feel if in 20 years' time we are still using technology in the same way? Unless we replace our problematic uses with uses that have a genuine positive impact, these unwanted effects will likely get worse.

This may not be your first effort towards resolving the emotional and mental tension that technology is causing us. Countless articles offer quick-fix solutions, often suggesting we stop using technology altogether. Self-help articles attribute our unhappiness and wellbeing issues to an addiction to technology, or to FOMO (fear of missing out). But the problem goes deeper than that. And unless you're moving to a deserted island with no wi-fi, simply eradicating technology is not a sustainable solution.

Many people tell me that they consistently pick up their device and use it without even realising. This worries them because they see that they have lost control.

The crux of our use of technology – and of our stress – is the intellectual and emotional reliance we have on it. We don't *talk* like this about any other object we own. This affects the way we understand ourselves, the world and our place in it. When our digital life is out of kilter this affects every aspect of our life – work, health, family, relationships.

This book is not a 'quick-fix' digital detox. It is based on evidence to help us achieve genuine, long-lasting change that will improve all areas of our life – for good.

In the coming chapters, we will explore how our digital lives tick, and the key reasons we reach for our devices when we do (even when we don't realise we're doing it). I'll share frank advice on where we are going wrong, and the practical tools we need to get it right, whether that's at home, at work or in our personal lives. I will bust some major toxic digital lifestyle myths, dissect every 'fad' solution we have been sold, and reset our thinking. I want us to have more time, feel more in control and understand how to use technology in a way that is empowering, not draining.

The digital dream?

In the last few years we have fallen into a technology-driven frenzy, furiously acquiring laptops, tablets, mobile phones, apps and social media accounts. The average 40-year-old now owns between three and five technology devices (often including a smartphone, tablet and laptop),[1] and spends 165 hours per month using technology.[2] That's 1980 hours, or three solid months we spend every year glued to our better half, aka our screen.

We advocate for protecting our earth, yet our obsession with having the latest devices means that we produce 53 million tonnes of e-waste each year.[3] That is equivalent in weight to 4500 Eiffel Towers – each year! There are public fears about technology 'addiction' and whether it's messing with our minds, yet we sleep overnight outside the store just so we can be the first to own a new model of phone. We've developed behaviours like taking our devices with us into the shower, and watching YouTube videos of people folding clothes to calm us.

The root cause of this has been our unwavering faith in the 'digital dream': the belief that technology will transform our life and improve it in ways we could barely comprehend.

We pursue this dream, desperate to 'keep up', despite not knowing exactly how our lives will be transformed or whether that transformation will actually be a good thing.

It's easy to think of the benefits of technology. Imagine not being able to quickly look something up online (perhaps how many episodes of *Seinfeld* were made, or how many Kardashian sisters there are). Picture not being able to send a text to your boss to let them know you're running late. *Stressful*, right? There might be real-world consequences if we decided to amputate technology from our lives.

Despite the obvious benefits, however, it's clear that the very thing that is enhancing our quality of life is coming at a cost.

Let me take you through the current state of play. Bear with me, there are a lot of statistics, but they're important – they give us a better idea of the ways our technology use is harming us, and how far-reaching those problems are.

Bedtime

Forget a good night's sleep. Life is different now!
Seventy-one per cent of adults sleep with their
phone either in their hand or within arm's reach.
Phone notifications mean 41 per cent of us have
an interrupted sleep most nights, and a whopping
12 per cent of adults deliberately wake up in the
middle of the night to use their phone.[4] Come
morning, 85 per cent of us reach for our phone as
the first movement of the day, and 50 per cent of
adults take their phone to the toilet.[5]

Work

The nine-to-five workday has been permanently
altered by technology. Multiple studies show that
the average adult checks their phone 76 times each
day.[6] That equates to around 2617 touches per day.[7]
We spend much of our working day switching from
website to app to social media to online shopping to
checking notifications, back to work. This is directly
affecting our productivity, our ability to focus deeply
on tasks, and our safety.

Technology has given us more autonomy in
defining our work hours, but it's also blurred the line
between work and life. For 65 per cent of us, this is

contributing to job stress and limiting our opportunities to rest.[8] We are struggling with information overload at work, and dealing with the constant change associated with work-related technology use.

Stress

Not only are we stressed because of technology, we also feel stress when we are *without* it. Fifty-two per cent of adults admit they don't want to be without their phone, and feel a sense of anxiety and withdrawal-like symptoms when they are away from it.[9] Problematic mobile phone use (PMPU) has been identified by the Australian Psychological Society as one of the biggest behavioural challenges of the twenty-first century.[10]

More than half of adults – 51 per cent – admit that they use technology as an emotional crutch to deal with stress.[11] That means that they reach for their device to avoid dealing with personal and professional issues. Sixty-five per cent of adults state that they would not cope without internet access for more than two consecutive hours.[12] Women report higher levels of techno-anxiety than men.

Family

As adults, we have messy digital lives, and many of us worry about what technology is doing to our kids.

The average teenager spends 45 hours per week on a screen, not including work or school.[13] Breaking it down, that's almost a third of each day. Children aged 8–12 years aren't far behind – they have around six hours of screen time per day. Even toddlers average 50 minutes per day, every day, on screens. Often this use starts at just a few months of age.

Any way you cut it, that's a lot of time to spend staring at a screen, especially for kids in their formative years. To counter this, we set timers, lock away devices and drone on about the importance of actual real-life human interaction. And then we check our phones.

To justify our actions and our loss of control, we blame the kids, or we blame the technology companies. But kids learn from us.

Intimacy

Hey, do you mind holding that orgasm for a moment? One in ten people admit to checking their phones during sex.[14] And among the 10 per cent of phone-checkers, 43 per cent are repeat offenders. And that's if we actually get to the point of having sex! According to a Lancaster University study, when people are in bed together they're doing a lot more Netflixing than sex these days.[15]

We've allowed technology to become a third wheel in our relationships, with many adults constantly competing with their partner's devices for time, attention and intimacy. This is creating conflict and leading to lower levels of relationship satisfaction.

Uses become habits

Most of the ways we use technology are habits we have unthinkingly fallen into. For example, did we decide to start spending long hours 'zombie scrolling' on our devices, or was it something we just seemed to start doing? Did we purposefully decide to start checking our device at inappropriate times, such as during sex, mid-conversation with our partner, or when our child is telling us something, or did it just start happening? Did we decide to film our major life events and upload them to social media, or did things like 'gender reveals' just start happening?

Did we make a conscious choice to
sleep with our phone under our pillow?
Why did these things just start happening?
Why do they keep happening?

The machine is winning

The digital world in which we live is a far cry from the utopia we have been promised. The race to get new products and services into the consumer marketplace gives little consideration to how these things may actually affect our quality of life. As a result, we have had to deal with the reality of living with these products, warts and all.

For example, Twitter was launched with little long-term planning to avoid its misuse, such as using it to sway major political events. Similarly, Artificial Intelligence (AI) has left the realm of science fiction and is now installed in the phone in our pocket, the laptop in our office and even the car that we drive. It has been sold to us as revolutionising efficiency, but it is steadily creeping in to control our choices. Listening to a song by Taylor Swift? Spotify will ensure that we get more of the same. Didn't finish watching that Netflix movie? AI will keep sending us notifications until we do.

Algorithms now determine passport control, the issuing of debt collection notices, home loans and insurance cover, who gets the job, even who will get targeted by police and how long their prison sentence might be. Political campaigns buy our data in order to produce targeted advertising for our personal habits and values.

AI is not a perfected science – it makes mistakes. Yet it holds power over us, and it's hard to argue against an AI bot. The machine wins. The human loses.

Our digital actions do not take place in a vacuum. They occur within this insatiable, constantly changing, technology-focused environment, where there is a lot of commercial gain and little accountability.

How many times a day do we flick away reminder notifications that we never asked for? How often have we had to change our work practices to accommodate new technology? How much online information is being collected about us every minute of every day without our permission? This is another layer of our digital life that can wear us down emotionally, physically, mentally and cognitively.

Changes keep happening, and it can seem like we are losing control. It's easy to feel overwhelmed by it all, but we risk falling into a defeatist groove.

A recent study in the United States found that 60 per cent of adults believe that it's not possible to avoid having their data collected by the technology industry and government, and admit they have no idea what either party does with it.[16] About 80 per cent believe that they have no control over the data collected, and that the potential risks of this data collection outweigh the potential benefits. Yet we continue to use the services of corporations we are suspicious of.

As a global groundswell of dissatisfaction builds, a technology backlash industry has sprung up to help us 'break up with our phones'. This takes the form of tech diets and social media accounts full of misleading 'inspirational' words. Screentime apps are peddled widely, with discounts on digital detox weekend retreats thrown in as a sweetener with every subscription. These retreats are often run by unqualified activists and 'wellness experts' – or, even better, by ex-Silicon Valley executives conjuring up their next business model.

Many tech companies have added wellbeing tools to their devices, but these tools haven't changed our habits. That's because they tell users what they are doing on their devices and for how long, but they do not provide the *why* – the intellectual and emotional reasons we use technology so obsessively. Half the time we pick up our phone it's in response to a notification. However, the other half of the time, there is no alert except the one inside our head telling us to check our phone.

We can't wait for Facebook or Google to rescue us. Technology companies are commercial organisations. They are designed to make money. Protecting us is starting to enter their field of vision, but money will always be their primary objective. What they have created is a massive beast, but expecting these multinationals to solve things for us will never be the solution.

Something has gone awry in our relationship with our ever-present devices. Our digital dream has turned into a digital nightmare.

As media theorist Marshall McLuhan commented, 'We shape our tools, and thereafter our tools shape us.' Technological innovation is faster than ever, which means that our tools are shaping us faster than ever. Just think, smartphones didn't exist ten years ago; now 2 billion people are using them – that's about a third of the earth's population. The way that has changed how we communicate, work and learn is astounding. And that's just one of the many devices we use.

We've been focused on the shape of our tools. On digital innovation. Now it's time to shift that focus to the behaviours and attitudes we've unconsciously taken on as a result of using these tools, and what impact they are having on us. We need to control our technological destiny before it controls us.

Shaping our digital reality

How can we find value and peace in lives when our ability to be productive, to be independent, to be protected, has been displaced by the digital tools and habits we've created?

The stress and pain technology causes us is tied to our reliance on it. If that reliance is unhealthy, then stress occurs.

We all use technology in individualised ways, and identifying which uses add value to our life and which cause us stress is important for our long-term digital happiness.

I'm still making changes in my own technology use all the time. I can unthinkingly pick up new digital habits, and it can be months before I realise the stress they are causing me. For example, I recently decided to use a new app to create my shopping lists. While it was convenient, it also led to me answering work emails while I was pushing the trolley. It took weeks before I realised why my grocery shopping had become so stressful!

Finding our digital groove means understanding what we do online, who with, when, where, how often, and for what purpose. We need a plan – one that focuses on how technology can create net value in our lives.

I want to start a movement that disrupts the way we use technology. I want us to have the principles to use technology in more positive and empowering ways, and to feel like they are second nature. They will liberate us. I've written this book with our struggles and stresses at the front of my mind. For each of us, there will be one breakthrough sentence or action point somewhere in this book that that will change our relationship with technology and improve every aspect of our life.

And no, I'm not going to suggest we should break up with technology. Trust me, there is a much better alternative.

It's time to reimagine our relationship with technology; to ask how we can use it to make our lives better. It's time to regain control and create our own digital dream. This is no longer a technology conversation. It's time to switch into 'life mode'. We need to focus on how technology lives with us, not the other way around.

Chapter 1

Digital fulfilment versus digital hypochondria

Different uses of technology have different effects on us. Some of these add value and some do not. There are lots of technology uses that people actually feel really good about. This is what I would call digital 'fulfilment'.

Here are some great examples of digital fulfilment:

`My 85-year-old dad uses Facebook to connect with kids and grandkids scattered across the country. Reading and commenting on their posts gives him the ability to participate in their lives.´

`My entertainment and reading options have exploded exponentially because of new technologies.´

`I joined my local neighbourhood Facebook group during lockdown and it has been a life changer! It's like rediscovering the idea of a community noticeboard.´

`Taking virtual tours of the best museums around the world – no airfare required.´

'I made a home video with my son on my phone. It was so good doing it together.'

'I phoned my mother to let her know I was running late, and it was so nice to have that ability.'

'Incredible communities have emerged online to give voice and community to those previously on the margins.'

'I'm learning to play a guitar from YouTube.'

'Instead of handwriting ALL the notes off the board, I take a photo of them and annotate the photo with my own notes.'

Albert Einstein remarked:

'Why does this magnificent applied science which saves work and makes life easier bring us so little happiness? The simple answer runs: because we have not yet learned to make sensible use of it.'

For too long, the idea of 'good' technology use has been linked to the idea of productivity; the assumption that with technology we will work faster and smarter, life will be better and we will be happier. And of course, new apps and devices mean that our life will be even *better* and we will be even *happier*.

These are not our ideas. These are the advertising dreams of the technology industry, and they are not working for us. Life isn't only about being more productive – and we don't even know if our current technology use actually does make us more productive!

Technology has ushered in a new way of life, but we haven't yet fully envisioned its purpose, meaning and opportunities. Despite what some companies might have us believe, we don't know how to live well with technology yet. Instead, we have fallen into ways we *think* we need to interact with technology, and this has left us feeling out of control and missing out on true digital fulfilment.

While Einstein of course wasn't talking about smartphones or laptops in the quote opposite, he was still right. It's not the technology itself that determines if we are happy, energised and calm, but how we use it.

My solution: change the way we think and act with technology, and this will change the effect it has on us.

Kick off change

There are three key starting points for kicking off this change. The first and most important is to shift the conversation from a 'technology' conversation to a 'life' conversation.

Technology should be something that serves us

How many of us buy new devices and apps, and fashion our life around them? It should be the other way around. This means figuring out the life we want and what would improve it, and then deciding how technology can help us do that.

This change in mindset reminds me of the backstory behind the video game Pokémon GO. When it was first developed, game manufacturers didn't believe that children wanted to go outside. They thought kids were happy inside on their screens. That was their running line, and it suited their business plan. Then here came this game that swept the world by storm – a game that has been downloaded over a billion times – that made children go outside. John Hanke, the inventor of the game, said he designed the game that way because he didn't like that feeling you get after you've been sitting around playing a video game for two or three hours. 'It feels exactly like you just ate a whole big bag of potato chips,' he said. He wanted to combine a video game with an active, outdoor experience that would leave you feeling refreshed. So he did. And it became a worldwide phenomenon.

I'm not telling you that you need to create a bestselling app. But you can shift your technology use to be more creative, and more focused on trying new things.

Digital fulfilment will be different for everyone
One of the great things about technology is that it offers us so many different resources and ways of using it. For this reason, we should never consider one single, rigid approach to digital practices that we should all adopt. Instead, I want to inspire you to explore options. The way we use technology right now is not the only way we can use it. I want to show you how to rethink your digital life.

Buying another app or device won't fix anything
Understanding why you use technology in the ways you do, and making changes based on that knowledge, is what will solve an unhealthy or draining relationship with technology.

Have you heard of these 'conditions'?

Binge-watching addiction: inability to turn off streaming services such as Netflix

Cyberchondria: feeling ill and anxious after searching online for symptoms of an illness

Cyberloafing: taking a micro break from housework, shopping or other activity by going online to check emails and social networks and search the internet

Digital detox: restricting or stopping technology use

Digital hypochondria: blaming technology use for the occurrence of complex health conditions

Digital hypochondria

The ideas we have about technology can get in the way of seeing the reality. Take 'internet addiction', for example. If you googled this term you'd be convinced that it is a thing. But it is not an actual disorder recognised by health professionals. It is not recognised in psychiatry manuals. It is not recognised by leading health authorities such as the World Health Organization (WHO) or the American Psychiatric Association (APA). Authentic, peer-reviewed scientific research is yet to agree that it is a real condition. Studies aren't presenting convincing evidence that excessive time spent on the internet is an addictive behavioural disorder. They show correlation, but they do not show causation. And that's a very different thing.

Because technology is changing so quickly, research cannot keep up. All research, including my own, takes a long time to be published in scientific journals. This means that the 'latest research' might actually be capturing our technology use three years ago.

So, in the absence of solid research evidence, fake 'advice' and scary unsubstantiated medical terms abound for conditions like 'cyberchondria' (feeling ill after searching online for symptoms of an illness) or 'nomophobia' (the fear of not being with your smartphone). I've put together a glossary of many of these contrived conditions throughout this chapter.

The condition 'selfitis' first appeared as a news story in a 'parody-style' publication.[17] Tongue-in-cheek, it was described as 'the obsessive compulsive desire to take photos of one's self and post them on social media'. The article claimed that the American Psychiatric Association had classed 'selfitis' as a new mental disorder.

The story was republished by news sites and social media around the world, without mentioning that it had been first published on a satirical website. It was taken seriously – some schools even taught lessons on it. Even though the term was fabricated, belief in the condition 'selfitis' has stuck.

Likewise, in 2020 'Breaking News' in the UK reported the first cases of 'Binge Watching Addiction'.[18] The report stated that three patients had sought help at a clinic after admitting that Netflix and other on-demand streaming services had taken over their lives. The article explained that a TV cliffhanger is a reward mechanism – like alcohol or drugs, it causes lack of sleep, hinders productivity and stops people from forming proper relationships.

The claim of a connection between TV cliffhangers and dopamine does have some truth in it. Dopamine is released by our brain whenever we experience anything that feels good, like hugging our kids or eating chocolate. Cues in our environment can also increase dopamine. A cliffhanger episode of a favourite TV series, combined with a glimpse of the next episode, can kick in the brain's wanting system, and can activate our brain's dopamine. This may lead us to watching the next episode in order to prolong that pleasure.

That, however, is not the evidence that we need to claim that binge-watching addiction is an actual condition.

The widespread belief in these fabricated conditions is having what I call a 'digital hypochondria' effect on us. It leads us to blame our child's depression on too much screen time, or to attribute the obesity crisis to too much time on our phones. These are complex health conditions, unlikely to have a single cause.

What these fabricated conditions have got going for them is that they are catchy terms, so are cited in media articles almost daily. The problem is that they draw our attention to the symptoms, not the causes.

Instead of focusing on the technology itself, we need to look at what leads us to use technology in ways that are causing us stress, and to change those behaviours. This may mean using technology less, or it may mean creating a more intentional and nurturing online environment and using it in more meaningful ways. Each change will bring you closer to ensuring that your technology use benefits your work, study, relationships, interests and life. This will help you take back control.

Fabricated conditions, real impacts

We often don't realise just how complex our technology use is, and research demonstrating this may be some years away. The way we use technology is ever-changing, and one study cannot uncover everything we need to know.

For instance, a study in the *Journal of Mental Health* found that girls who use social media a lot are more likely to be depressed.[19] However, it's impossible to tell from this one study whether girls who use social media become depressed, or whether girls who are depressed are more likely to use social media – you can't say whether it's a symptom or a cause. It's plausible that social media

Perhaps you've diagnosed yourself with:

Doxxing: maliciously publishing private information about an individual online

FOMO: fear of missing out

Internet addiction: uncontrolled use of the internet

Nomophobia: the fear of not being with your smartphone

PMPU: problematic mobile phone use; a condition identified by the Australian Psychological Society as one of the biggest behavioural addiction challenges of the twenty-first century use could exacerbate pre-existing symptoms of depression, but it's impossible, from this study or most others, to know for sure. Only many studies, combined can make this clear.

In the absence of scientific research, conditions such as internet addiction have gained acceptance as a real thing. Many of us would jokingly say that we are addicted to the internet. But even though this is not a real medical condition, people are diagnosing it freely, and treating it however they choose to. They may merely be treating a symptom and leaving the real and underlying problem unresolved.

Consider going to the doctor and being diagnosed with a condition, only to find that there is no such illness. What criteria did the doctor use to diagnose you?

On what basis did they prescribe the medicine? How might this diagnosis affect you? Will it resolve your actual health condition or make it worse? Are they taking advantage of your lack of medical knowledge?

We have seen this in questionable treatments of internet addiction. Camps have popped up in China and other parts of the world claiming to stop teenagers becoming addicted to technology. These camps are for-profit, and sometimes use military-style corporal punishment and electric shock therapy as a 'cure' for alleged internet addiction in adolescents. Marketing for such camps declared that electric shock therapy was only painful for those with internet addiction – experiencing pain meant that your child was being cured.[20]

These treatments, which are based on unsubstantiated claims, give people false hope and take advantage of desperate parents and adolescents. There have been multiple deaths in these camps. Thankfully, in 2017 a new law was passed by the Chinese Ministry of Health to end the use of electroshock therapy as a 'cure' for this fabricated condition.[21]

Self-diagnosis isn't limited to technology 'conditions'. Say you've been having stomach pains. You don't go to the doctor, but you do some research online and conclude that you have an intolerance to eggs. You start to shape your life around this apparent intolerance. You stop eating cakes, change your breakfast and so on. You've never actually asked the doctor about it, but you've convinced yourself you have an intolerance. But do you? And what impact could your behaviour be having on your health and your life?

Buzzword or real condition?

Selfitis: the obsessive-compulsive desire to take photos of one's self and post them on social media

Techno-anxiety: anxiety and withdrawal-like symptoms when away from one's phone

Technostress: difficulty in managing the collision between technology-related work demands and life. Proven symptoms include fatigue, irritability, insomnia, a sense of ineffectiveness and a reduction in job satisfaction and employee commitment.

The symptom, not the cause

What research *is* finding is that uncontrolled technology use is not necessarily caused by technology. It makes sense, when you think about it. People don't think that people who sleep all day have a 'bed addiction'. Studies are finding that extreme technology use is generally a symptom of another, underlying disorder such as depression, anxiety or attention problems. Just as a person may turn to alcohol or drugs when they are struggling to cope, they can also turn to video games or other technology use.

There was substantial backlash from the health industry when the World Health Organization officially classified an addiction to video games as 'gaming disorder'. They defined this disorder as 'impaired control over gaming, increasing priority given to gaming over other activities to the extent that gaming takes precedence over other interests and daily activities, and continuation or escalation of gaming despite the occurrence of negative consequences'.[22]

Many authorities, including the Media Psychology and Technology division of the American Psychological Association, stated that the WHO seemed to ignore the body of research that suggested 'gaming disorder' is more likely to be a symptom of other, underlying mental health issues such as depression. The WHO's sister organisation, UNICEF, also argued against using this language to describe children's screen use, expressing concern that this could set a child up to think they have an addiction when they do not.[23]

A mother of a 15-year-old girl once told me, 'My daughter is addicted to her phone.' When I asked her how she knew this, she said, 'Because she's always holding it. And everything you read tells us that this generation of kids are addicted. All of them. It's so hard being a parent now. I'm so glad I'm not a kid today.'

She isn't the only parent who has told me that their child has a technology addiction. I would say that over 70 per cent of parents I speak to tell me the same thing.

Think about the implications of a parent saying this to their child. What message are they actually sending about technology? What message are they sending about health and wellbeing? Does the parent provide any hope or strategies for changing the child's relationship with technology (which, of course, is likely to play an increasing role in that child's life)? And is the parent role-modelling better behaviour in the first place?

Most of the conditions described in this chapter are not backed by the evidence that they should be. But that doesn't mean that we can't relate to them in some way – we do.

Many of us feel that we've lost control of our technology use and we want to gain balance. I want to arm you with a new way of thinking, new perspectives. True digital wellness is about creating balance.

Get the facts

Finding information about health and wellbeing is easy. Cutting through the clutter and getting the facts, however, is very difficult.

We are constantly bombarded with contradictory information about technology. 'Technology makes us obese', 'Technology will help your child learn better', 'Technology causes violent behaviour', 'Technology gives us the career edge'. Fake news and disinformation are becoming increasingly widespread, making it difficult for the general public to separate reliable information from misleading content. In this state of play, it's easy to be swayed by pseudoscience.

It's always really important to be critical of where information is coming from. Any argument can sound convincing if you don't dig into the science behind it. Remember, 'clinically proven' means nothing at all. If an article can't point us to the research backing up the claims, it's worthless, and is manipulating us. That's why I've included endnotes in this book. They provide real evidence. Use them to follow up on what you'd like to know more about.

I spend a lot of my day wading through all kinds of literature, so I've developed a good bullshit radar. There's a lot of rubbish out there dressed up as real science. Here are some warning signs that something is probably junk instead of fact.

- Only one study or one person's story is used to convince us, or the information is based solely on testimonials and anecdotes.

- Research or science is alluded to, but no actual references to reputable journal studies are provided.

- You are encouraged to spend money on products or services to achieve the lifestyle that's being promoted.

For example, one article about binge-watching addiction was printed alongside an advertisement for a new subscription service that claimed to offset Netflix addiction using the calming presence of plants. Bullshit alert activated.

Throughout this book I'd like you to challenge your own beliefs about our technology use and the information that you have come to accept as true. And next time you read about a digital health condition, I want you to look for red flags.

A new vocabulary

This technology-fuelled life is new to us, and can sometimes feel out of control. Finding meaning and a path is important. There is a lot of fearmongering around digital hypochondria. As a result, we live with this gloom, stuck in the belief that we have no hope of changing our technology use. But that's not the case.

Forget 'selfitis', 'internet addiction', 'binge-watching addiction' or 'nomophobia'. Let's create our own terms, like 'digi-creativity' and 'technogood'. Terms that don't feed on fear but that build empowerment, and focus on owning our actions and achieving balance and peace.

Some new terms for new uses:

Digi-creativity: using technology to explore creative ideas, develop creative thinking skills, and create new art forms

Cyber-belonging: technology uses that foster a sense of belonging and that create meaningful interactions with others

RDE (real digital evidence): reliable evidence to support the explanation of a digital practice or problem

Technogood: uses of technology that create a more positive world

Digital fulfilment: technology uses that people feel really good about

Good technology use

So, if good technology use doesn't mean restricting your time on your device, what *does* it mean? I'll provide many explanations of digital fulfilment over coming chapters, but I'd like to start with this one.

In 2020, Australia experienced the most devasting bushfires this planet has seen. We often think of social media in divisive terms –the never-ending pursuit of 'likes', or the mental health issues caused by social comparison. But these heartbreaking bushfires saw social media become a space of comfort that brought the community together.

Status updates were used to reassure worried friends and family, 'I'm okay'. Videos shot on people's phones gave us insight into the devastation and pain people were facing, firsthand. An online campaign raised more than $18 million for volunteer firefighters in just two days. Hundreds of thousands of people from around the world pledged millions of dollars. This showed humanity at its best, and provided a perfect example of good and empowering technology use.

In a crisis, social media becomes an emotional conduit. Those at the centre of the disaster share posts as a way of dealing with the tragedy, and we respond by sharing our support and empathy.

But social media doesn't do this – we do this. It is our use of the tools that social media provides that makes it happen.

Too often, the concept of personal happiness is left out of discussions about technology, when the opposite should be the case. Technology has become such a big part of our lives, it's vital that we discuss how it links to our happiness.

We all come to our happiness from different places, with different values and desires. But what goes without saying for all of us is that our actions and practices have a big impact on our happiness. A study by the University of California found that happiness is determined by three factors: our genetics (50 per cent), our circumstances (10 per cent), and our activities and practices (40 per cent). That means that 40 per cent of our happiness is determined by the choices we make.

Happiness is not a one-dimensional, fixed concept, and neither is any feeling of wellbeing that we can gain from technology. Good technology use isn't just about staying off our devices after 9 pm. It's about using technology to enhance our sense of belonging, to build warm, satisfying and trusting relationships, to support our personal needs and values, to help us work and live independently and productively, to enhance our life in ways that we value, to achieve goals and to continue to learn and grow.

If every day you used your phone in one way that genuinely makes you feel good, what difference do you think this approach would have on your life? For example, 'Today I am going to take 15 minutes to try a new drawing app,' or 'My kid loves to play a music game online. I usually complain about this, but today I'm going to join him and have some fun.' What difference would this value-add approach have?

Digital restriction is not digital liberation

Paradoxically, we are simultaneously under enormous pressure to be online but also to take control and resist being online. We clearly can't give in to both pressures and be happy or healthy.

No wonder there has been a massive upsurge of products and services that are designed to ensure we use technology less. These range from digital detox 'spa days' that include therapies, mindfulness sessions and wellness cuisine, to remote 'cold turkey' cabins where your device is physically locked away at check-in. There are also apps that lock down your device for a designated period of time, and charge you a fee to access it before that time is up.

The problem is that using technology less, or not at all, is neither desirable nor sustainable. I get frustrated with pseudo solutions such as digital detoxes because they suggest that we can only feel happy and healthy if we don't use technology at all; that a perfect life is a life without a screen.

But we don't live in the eighteenth century. Technology is integrated in almost every part of our life – our work, school and social lives. For many of us, going without it just isn't an option.

One major issue with screen restriction methods is that they fail to tell us how we are actually supposed to work and function screenless. Besides, going cold turkey is rarely the best way to kick a habit. You may use your technology less on the weekend, but what happens on Monday? Research consistently shows that we fall back into the same habits that were causing us stress before our digital-free period.[24] They offer no solution, they simply put the problem on pause.

The problem isn't necessarily with the crying baby; it's that we pick the baby up every time it cries.

The core of our issue is not our phone, laptop, smartwatch, social media or the internet itself. We are being sidetracked by the idea that we must eradicate technology, when really we need to be focusing on how we use it.

Take action: the five principles for digital fulfilment

The aim of this book is to help change our mindset from digital illness to digital wellness.

I love this quote from William Arthur Ward: 'The pessimist complains about the wind; the optimist expects it to change; the realist adjusts the sails.'

I'm proposing a new way of thinking, a new philosophy for a happy and fulfilling life – with screens. And to help establish this new philosophy, I'm calling on an old one. Aristotle's term 'eudaimonia' (pronounced u-day-monia) translates to 'human flourishing'. We flourish when we have a life of purpose and direction. This means stepping off that doomscrolling path and doing meaningful things with technology instead. Because, as we know, this is not just a technology conversation. This is a life conversation.

The following five principles for digital fulfilment are at the core of this new philosophy, and will be central to the rest of this book.

1. Understand that technology can be a tool to enhance life. This is not only a real possibility, it's a necessity.

2. Know your habits. We need to look beyond the act of picking up the phone, and consider why we picked it up.

3. Know your context. The tricks technology companies use to keep us hooked, and the culture and distraction that might be at play in our office spaces, are just some of the factors in our environment that influence our technology use.

4. Recognise opportunities. Rather than trying to 'fix' the problems with our technology behaviour, let's shift our thinking to consider which technology uses can bring us fulfilment.

5. Set goals. This is our life, not our laptop's life. Put yourself first and identify some things that you'd like to achieve or change in your life, and work out how technology can help with that.

Chapter 2

Digital superhumans?

Humans have been trying to enhance our physical and mental capabilities for thousands of years. We have designed numerous tools to free ourselves from the limits of being 'human'. Planes to help us fly, wheels to let us travel faster, tools to make us strong, make-up and surgery to enhance our appearance.

And then along came smart devices – the ultimate human enhancer.

Technology offers us so many functions to provide the help we want when we want it. Need to message your work team? Just say the word. Need to translate the menu in an overseas restaurant? Got it. Need to test the air quality because you're asthmatic? Use this app. It would have been near impossible to contain outbreaks of Covid-19 without our use of contact tracing apps.

And now that our devices are mobile, we never need to be without them.

> The opportunities our devices provide are endless. Not even your best friend or your partner can provide that level of assistance and support.

Life-tracking apps give us insight into our health, in a way that we as non-doctors have never been able to access before.[25] An app that tracks our heart rhythm can provide insight into our heart rate performance over time – the app automatically records irregularities to inform cardiology treatment. This information gives us greater awareness of how our bodies function, and can help us ask better questions of our doctors. A menstrual cycle tracking app can help us understand the connection between our cycle and our moods. This insight can help us deal with the corresponding mood in a different and possibly better way.

As a researcher and writer, my smart device is integral to my work. I could not be as productive without it. I have a photo album on my phone called 'Good ideas'. This album contains screenshots of notes, paragraphs of books, articles, diagrams and headlines that have stimulated new thinking for me. I use the content of this album when I'm writing, planning to give a keynote, planning a workshop. I've used it many times while writing this book. There is no way I could remember all of these ideas without these digital prompts!

We are the first humans in history to have this kind of enhancement. It's no wonder technology is having such an impact on us. The mental and emotional protection we gain from our devices feels so good, we don't want to be without them.

This is apparent in the way we treat our devices. Many of us would admit to feeling anxious when they are not close by. We keep them in our pocket or our handbag; if we move to another room, we take our

Over time, we've actually fashioned technology into an external brain that we use to help us function better mentally. This is sometimes referred to as the 'extended mind'.

phone with us. I know a man who takes his laptop everywhere he goes. To a restaurant, to the beach, to a concert. He admits it's heavy and an inconvenience, but he wants it by his side.

We justify our fixation. We say, 'What if the kids need me?' or, 'What if my boss calls?' Many people believe that FOMO is the reason we don't want to be without our devices, but FOMO is a poor metric for understanding our relationship with technology.

The fact is, day after day we use technology to boost our capabilities on a massive scale. The boost it gives us, both intellectually and emotionally, is unrivalled. Technology is the extension of ourselves that makes us feel superhuman. Knowing the reliance we have on it, and why, is an important step towards changing our practices for the better.

The extended mind

One of the most alluring aspects of technology is that it makes us feel and act smarter. I don't mean it's like carrying around a textbook with new facts and figures we can use. The intellectual confidence our technology gives us is much more intimate and, some may say, even a little creepy. Our 'extended mind' gives us a huge boost, but it also creates many tensions for us.

Have you ever done any of the following?

'When having dinner with friends I often look up a piece of information to settle a discussion. For example, when did Prince William and Kate get married? Oh, that's right: April 2011.'

'If I'm asked to choose a restaurant in an unfamiliar location, I check a restaurant app to select a venue with good reviews.'

'I'm studying, and sometimes feel overwhelmed by the course materials. In the seminar room I will take a photo of the study notes on the whiteboard so I can refer to them later.'

'On the way to coffee at a friend's house, I use a map app for directions, even if I've maybe been there once or twice before.'

'I use my online calendar across all my devices to organise my day – on my phone to wake me up, on my laptop to keep my daily schedule, and on my smartwatch to text work colleagues throughout the day.'

Using technology in any of these ways means that we're using it to boost our cognitive and brain functioning. We're using it to help us remember, learn, problem-solve, make decisions and connect with friends. We do this seamlessly, moving between our human brain and our digital brain often without even realising it's happening.

Supersized memory

An important part of our ability to solve problems is our capacity to remember. You need to remember the facts and information before you can apply them to the problem at hand.

But forgetful days are a thing of the past.

Our devices have become our personalised information storage systems. They're where we store the notes from the seminar we went to last year, the beginning ideas for the report we're writing, the steps for how to get into our new apartment building, the phone number of the person we met yesterday. We even put a reminder in our phone to ensure we call them.

Thanks to technology, we now outsource our memory, or part of it, to our devices.

Once upon a time we would have jotted down ideas in a notebook. Our devices have blown this out of the water.

Sometimes we take a photo for future reference, ask Siri to remind us about the facts and figures we want to remember, or drop pins in our online map to remember where we parked our car. We store this information in whatever form is the most convenient for us to recall it when we need it. This depends on how much there is, and how much we need to remember.

Have you ever turned up to work when you weren't at your best? Maybe you'd been up all night with a crying baby, or you were sick, or you'd had an argument with your partner. Feeling tired, stressed or filled with emotion can lead to memory decline. On those days, we tend to rely on our digital brain to do the heavy lifting for us. To help us be organised, solve problems and generally get things done. When things turn around and we're feeling more capable, we mightn't need our technology as much for this purpose. It provides us with the boost we need when we need it. We feel intellectually secure because we can access our 'internet brain' whenever we need a bit of cognitive propping up.

Using technology to support our memory can free up our brain space for more creative problem-solving. Some studies show that using it in this way actually levels the playing field between people with different cognitive skill levels.[26]

It's not all rosy, though. The more we rely on technology in this way, the less able we will actually be to remember information.

Research has found that people who rely on technology for recall have lower rates of recall of the information itself, but an enhanced recall for where to access it.[27] You can't remember the date of your cousin's birthday, but you know where you've stored this information on your phone.

Just as muscles need training to grow, our brain needs training, particularly in childhood. Heavily outsourcing mental activity to a device can potentially hinder our ability to learn. This is a huge problem for children, as it can impact their learning well into adulthood.

I will keep saying this: it's *how* we use technology that is important, not *how much*. The key here is not necessarily where the information is stored but how we interact with it. This does not mean children (or adults) shouldn't use technology to store information, but it does mean we need to use the information we have stored for creative and problem-solving activities, as these experiences give our brain a workout.

I'm right again!

There's one more important layer to our digital 'superhumanity'. Our devices make us think we know more than we do. That's right – technology makes us think and act like we are actually smarter.

We don't think of the information we're seeing on Google as something sourced outside of our own brain. We think of it as knowledge that we possess.

We don't claim ownership of the things we learn when we read a book or newspaper; we only do it with online information. And there's a reason for this crazy, weird phenomenon.

Our smart devices provide us with almost immediate access to an unparalleled amount of information that we carry around 24/7. It's in our pocket or beside us when we work, eat dinner, walk the dog. Many of us even shower with that information.

Plus, there is no expectation that we must remember any of it – we can access these facts and figures any time.

Research shows that this combination of factors is feeding a sense of intellectual arrogance, and an unprecedented emotional bond with our device. It makes us feel like the new information is 'ours'.

Supersizing our brain using technology gives us the confidence to do things that moments ago we knew little or nothing about.

Jack watched one YouTube video showing him how to change the alternator on his car. He had no prior knowledge of mechanics, and he didn't have a teacher or friend to show him what to do. But he did it – with the assistance of his trusty device.

Our smart devices remove the limits to what we think we know and can do. This moves us into that superhuman realm. Technology is our Ironman suit. It can be a huge booster for our confidence, and this is another reason we don't want to be without it.

This all sounds pretty good, and in some ways, it is. But the fact is, we've never had to manage such a complex and seductive object as technology before. It's like taming a wild horse.

And to make it even more challenging, while we're trying to come to grips with this, others (including the technology companies) are manipulating the horse in ways that we're not aware of.

The support we want from technology differs for everyone. It depends on a range of factors, including our location, whether it's a weekday or weekend, our lifestyle, age and personality.

Everyone has a friend who's always looking up the 'right answer' to win an argument.

'Bican has scored more goals than any other soccer player.'

'No way. It's gotta be Ronaldo.'

'Want to bet?'

'I'll google it.'

Whether they're discussing the correct way to do a push-up or how often a dog should be washed, some people will insist they are correct, and they'll turn to Google to prove it.

Let me explain this using the latest psychological research.[28] Think about a time you've heard an expert being interviewed. They are usually very sure of and fixed in their knowledge. They have already given extensive thought to issues within their particular domain, and have 'earned' the privilege of harbouring set opinions and beliefs.

From a psychological point of view, people are more influenced by the behaviour of experts than by the content they provide. So individuals who believe they are experts (or want us to believe they are) tend to overestimate the accuracy of their beliefs. Like real experts, they become certain that their knowledge is correct. Google is their ultimate tool to endorse this and convince us.

A wannabe expert is going to develop an even greater emotional reliance on technology. This can sometimes lead to an inflated intellectual ego and an unrealistic sense of self. Technology aside, the reason some people want to win every argument is not related to their laptop or phone, but to other factors, including their disposition and their self-esteem. Technology can mask these issues, both for the individual and others.

We all do this sometimes – we use our internet IQ to challenge a situation. Maybe we're not sure the plumber is fixing our shower properly, so we jump online and, armed with fresh 'knowledge', we question their work. Perhaps we've queried legal documents despite not being a lawyer.

Right or wrong, the superhuman feeling we get from technology affects the way we treat others and the value we attribute to knowledge that is in our own pocket. We can become the intellectual bully in the playground.

Survival instincts

Regarding information that we've sourced online as our own is bizarre, or even arrogant, but it could also be a tendency that we've developed to survive in today's digital world. Think about it from this perspective: we live in an era that relies on knowledge, and when used well, technology relieves the pressure to know and remember everything.

Humans have long developed tools to enhance their survival. Our ancestors learned to expertly combine flint and sticks to create fire. This dramatically improved their quality of life in a physically demanding environment. In a sense, we are doing the same thing.

Modern-day humans are simply evolving to outsource our information needs. This allows us to thrive in today's harsh intellectual environment.

How could we even come close to meeting our enormous knowledge demands without virtual help? With the volume of available information growing constantly, being able to locate it on demand becomes a necessity. This only strengthens the emotional connection we have with our devices.

Of course, our ability to extend our mental capability depends on the site or app we've chosen to use. If you've ever ruined your hair by following a dodgy 'blonde highlights at home' video, you'll know what I mean.

Applying digital knowledge to our real-world lives becomes so automatic that we can sometimes make dubious decisions about which advice to follow. Our survival instincts aren't always spot on.

Now-defunct wellness 'influencer' Belle Gibson was fined $400,000 for misleading her online followers with claims that she had cured herself of brain cancer through alternative therapies and nutrition.[29] Her wellness app was based on her healing process, and 300,000 people bought it. But it turned out she had never actually had the disease, and the court found her health advice to be shonky and dangerous.

We look to the internet for answers, for protection. Self-diagnosing a health condition that you know nothing about can lead to anxiety, misdiagnosis and 'cyberchondria'.[30] One study tracked 515 individuals in their health-related searches.[31] They found that searches of common, harmless symptoms often led to people self-diagnosing something much more serious and rare. For example, a headache might be diagnosed as a brain tumour (instead of the much more likely condition of caffeine withdrawal), muscle twitches as Lou Gehrig's disease (probably just benign muscle strain) and chest pain as heart attack (instead of indigestion or heartburn).

Two factors are at play here. One, search algorithms tend to display more serious illnesses in their results, and two, as humans we have a tendency to overstate how sick we actually are.

> Every superhero needs to understand their vulnerabilities and threats.

Intellectual arrogance comes from closing ourselves off to new ideas. However, if we can utilise discovered information to open new ways of thinking and problem-solving, we can truly unlock the potential of technology to help us innovate and arrive at new solutions.

As the volume of available information grows each day, being able to locate it as we need it becomes vital. Our digital brain should not be about arrogance or feeding an over-inflated sense of self – it's about surviving and thriving.

Emotional security

As part of my work, I interview a lot of children. One of the things I have discovered is that children gain emotional security from using a smart device because it can feel like an adult is always nearby.

I once had a six-year-old boy tell me that the voice assistant on his tablet was his best friend. 'She helps me with my homework, answers questions about what I want to know. She tells me stories and jokes.'

The boy had a loving and supportive home life. However, the adult voice and adult-like presence of his voice assistant made him feel secure. Children of this age can ask a lot of questions, and in the boy's eyes, Siri was like a substitute grown-up, always there when he needed answers. In line with all artificial intelligence, the more Siri adapts to his preferences, the more comforting, human-like qualities he will attribute to her. This will strengthen his emotional bond with his device.

It's not the individual devices that we have an emotional connection with, it's the functionality that they provide. When we upgrade to a new phone or laptop, we automatically transfer our emotional bond to the new device.

The newer the model, the greater the functionality, and the more promise it holds for us to be superhuman. We don't do this with other loved objects (or people); we retain our connection to them, even if they might no longer be really 'useful' to us.

For many of us our smartphone is our standout security blanket. Research from Columbia University shows that when we feel challenged or uncomfortable, most of us reach for our phone – over any other object we possess – for comfort.[32] Further research shows that our zombie scrolling becomes especially pronounced when we are undergoing stressful life changes, such as quitting smoking, or dieting.[33]

We also customise our phone to relieve our stress. We put the apps we use to escape in easy-to-access spaces on our screen, and our wallpapers feature our loved ones or special places, making the device more comforting. We even give it a name or speak about it as if it is a friend or family member.

As a result, our own phone relieves stress to a greater extent than an identical brand and model of phone that belongs to someone else, and more than any other device we might own, such as a laptop or desktop.

A Korean study examining the emotional bond humans form with their smartphones found that of the 60 adults interviewed, 30 per cent expressed a feeling of friendship towards their phone, or said it gave them the sense of another intelligent being's presence.[34]

One 30-year-old female participant said, 'My smartphone is my closest friend and I am the closest friend to my smartphone. It's like the smartphone is something like a friend living in myself. I live with my phone all the time; it never leaves me.' Similarly, a 27-year-old male participant said, 'After two years of trying, I finally landed a job I wanted to get. The first thing I did after receiving the acceptance call was to kiss my phone. In such a joy, unwittingly I called my phone by my name. And I hugged it for more than 5 minutes and kissed it more than a dozen times.' In his excitement, this man thought of his phone as both a friend and as an equivalent self.

Just like a toddler wants
their teddy, we want our phone.
It makes us feel safe.

Take action: knowledge is power

Our relationship with technology has become one of the most significant in our lives. However, we've never had to manage a relationship with an object like this before – one that is so enticing, demanding and complex.

Greek philosopher Heraclitus put it eloquently over two millennia ago: 'Nothing new comes into our lives without a hidden curse.' The greater the marvel, the greater the unexpected consequences.

Awareness that technology makes us feel superhuman, and an understanding of the emotional security this gives us, can help mitigate the lack of control we can feel with our devices.

We can enhance our control by noticing whether certain situations trigger greater emotional reliance on our device. Do you turn to your device to seek reassurance in particular situations, such as trouble at work or drama with friends? When you are feeling unwell or emotional, do you turn to your phone to make you feel better? Have you decorated your devices with photos of people and places you love to enhance its role as a source of emotional comfort?

Balancing out control also comes from thinking about the strategies you use to boost yourself intellectually. In line with Heraclitus, one of the hidden curses of the internet is the enormous amount of misinformation online that can trip us up. If we want to use technology to boost our capacity, then it's vital that we use information that is correct, and sites and people online who are trustworthy.

Chapter 3

Digital empowerment

Technology is not inherently good or bad for you. Both successful people and those who accomplish nothing use technology. Both happy and unhappy people use technology. Both stressed and unstressed people use technology. Both burnt-out people and those who are flourishing use technology.

The key point of difference is the differing habits people develop in their technology use. Have we ever taken a step back to really think about our own technology practices, to identify which uses are causing us stress and why?

Each and every one of us should know which uses of technology work well for us and which are causing us stress, pain and unhappiness.

This means looking beyond the act of picking up our phone and really considering *why* we picked it up. It means looking beyond the act of zombie scrolling social media to ask why we are doing this. I want us all to walk away from this chapter armed with the knowledge and confidence to scrutinise our actions with technology. This is key to creating a happier digital you.

We've already started to explore the emotional relationship we have with technology, which is rooted in the ability of our devices to make us feel superhuman. But that emotional connection goes deeper.

The number one reason
we feel burnt out from our
technology use is because we use
it to escape our stress. It's the junk
food of our digital world.

Do any of the following examples sound familiar?

'I scroll Instagram to stop myself from worrying about the argument I had with my partner.'

'My phone is a way for me to get away and distract myself, instead of sitting there stressed out because I just argued with a customer.'

'When I get angry, I pick up my phone. It helps me cool down and stops me from saying something I'll regret.'

'Every time I want a cigarette, I pull out my phone and scroll.'

'I was so tired today. So I ended up using apps and games to uplift myself and relax.'

'Whenever I get bored at work I check my phone. Sometimes I don't even realise I'm doing it. I do a bit of work, then check my phone. Do a bit more work, then back on my phone. That's pretty much what I do every day.'

'I didn't feel like cleaning up, so I hopped online to see what people are doing.'

'I feel awkward out in public so I scroll Facebook. I look like I'm busy, but I kind of waste time sitting there, looking at pictures and videos.'

We turn to our devices to instantly relieve or replace any part of ourselves that we experience as a problem, inadequacy or that we feel is missing in our life.

We might use our device to escape from something internally, such as a negative emotion, boredom or low energy. Or we might use it to escape from something external, like a dispute at work or feeling awkward when alone in a crowd, relationship problems or arguments with the kids.

Some of these issues are impacted by more serious conditions, of course. But it's good to recognise if we're using our phone to avoid dealing with them, and to recognise that this won't help!

Uncontrolled scrolling

I know you might be thinking, 'But life isn't all rosy. Some days are downers. Chilling out on your phone for a bit of relief can't be that bad for you.'

Sure, but the issue is that we aren't doing this every now and then. We are doing this every day. Multiple times, every single day.

And this escape comes with a catch. It might feel comforting to check our device, but repeatedly doing this has made us more prone to low-level addictive behaviours.

In my research I've found that addictive types of screen behaviours occur when we repeatedly use technology in ways that have no real purpose. Say you're waiting in line and you're bored, so you pull out your phone. You're tired or lonely, so you pull out your device. You're not using technology in any purposeful way, but the act of using technology makes you feel better.

The more we use technology to fill in the low moments, the more likely this is to become a habit. Absentmindedly checking our device becomes a 'normal' part of our day. We've got to the point where we now check our screen every 10 minutes – often without even realising that we're doing so.[35]

> Almost all of us single out passive scrolling as the digital behaviour we want to stop. It makes us feel empty and as though we've lost control.

Sometimes we start using our device with the best of intentions, but quickly forget them. A man told me that he promised his girlfriend he wouldn't check Facebook while they watched a movie together, but then ten minutes later, without even realising it, his phone was

It's a catch-22 situation.
The more we use technology
to escape, the less confident
we feel in successfully resolving
the lulls we encounter.

back in his hand. She said, 'You said you weren't going to use your phone!' He said, 'Oh, yeah, right, I forgot,' then put his phone back down.

Escaping into our screen when we experience a problem can become an automatic response. You have a confrontation with a work colleague and dive into your Instagram feed. This delays you resolving the issue, or means you avoid doing so altogether.

Our devices are always with us, and this can feed the mindset that escape is easy. But more intentional use feeds more control, and has a more positive impact. Habitual and passive behaviour leads to *more stress*.

In fact, most of us feel physically and mentally tired and drained *because* of passive scrolling on our device – the exact behaviour that we hope will ease our worries. This same technology use makes us feel less productive, less thoughtful, and less capable of asserting any agency. And it's taking a toll on our relationships.

Like eating junk food, scrolling your phone is attractive in the now, but in the aftermath it doesn't feel as powerful. Our technology use is clouding our brain and dissipating our focus. We make better decisions when we think, *How do I want to feel tomorrow?* instead of, *How do I want to feel right now?*

Living well with technology is not about screen-time bargaining. We need to understand what we really want or crave, and how we are using technology as a substitute for it.

Managing distraction is about managing pain and emotion, not managing the notification settings on your iPhone. Sure, doing that helps, but not if you can't manage the pain and discomfort that's driving you to your phone in the first place.

Aristotle's idea of eudaimonia suggests that wellbeing is more than just striving for maximum pleasure and minimum pain; it's about a sense of fulfilment and meaning. Not everything that makes us happy makes us feel fulfilled.

Scrolling through pictures of adorable puppies might cheer us up, but it won't feel meaningful. What gives us meaning in life are experiences that focus on self-acceptance, personal growth, purpose, positive relations with others, and the ability and autonomy to manage our life and surrounding environment.

Meaningful activity is one of the key factors that influences our mental health. The association between meaningful activity and the boost it gives our health and wellbeing is well documented. Having meaning improves our mood, helps combat depression and anxiety, improves the quality of our sleep, combats loneliness, builds our sense of self-worth and gives us satisfaction.

We are currently on the brink of a mental health crisis, and our repetitive 'escapist' technology use is not helping. Technology is an important part of our lives, but we need to direct meaning into our uses of it.

The opposite of stressful technology use is not use that makes us laugh or feel happy, it is use that gives us meaning, that makes us grow and feel better as a person.

This means ditching our short-term, instant-gratification use, and instead pursuing use that is actually going to benefit us tomorrow and the next day. It's like choosing healthy food over junk food.

Healthy use is intentional use

Habitual, passive scrolling is what pulls us into fragility and a loss of autonomy, but intentional and meaningful use is what pulls us out. We can think of this in relation to the key aspects of our technology use. Here are some strategies to consider.

Be intentional in your device set-up
This means being conscious of the physical factors that affect our technology use, such as the devices we own and where we keep them.

Many of us are in the habit of always keeping our phone screen visible and 'awake'. In a cafe, our phones are usually on the table, screen facing up. When we're pushing the kids on a swing, our phones are in our pockets. When going to sleep, we tuck our phone within arm's reach.

These routines have become the norm. Phones are small and easily tucked in wherever we go. In doing this, the message we are giving ourselves is that we need to act like first responders and jump on any notification as soon as it arrives. In reality, there is no urgency. We are creating that immediacy ourselves.

Be mindful of the routines you've established that are actually junk food habits.

Buy an alarm clock. Don't be one of the 41 per cent who regularly have an interrupted sleep due to phone notifications.

If you have more than one device, nominate one for work and the other for downtime.

If you move from one room to the next and take your phone with you, ask yourself why. What is it that you are waiting for? If you can't think of a legitimate reason, consider adjusting this routine.

These changes are small, but they help you to separate activities – asleep and awake, work and play, need phone and don't need phone. Separating our physical device set-up in this way keeps our technology use focused and intentional.

But one of the biggest mistakes we make is to make changes only to our physical use of technology and assume that will improve our digital habits. Reducing the negative impact of technology means moving beyond the physical use of our devices.

Be intentional in your device floor plan

When we move into a new home, we design and arrange our furniture to suit a particular lifestyle. If you love cooking, then your kitchen will look different to that of someone who can barely boil an egg. The set-up would determine how much time you spend in the kitchen and how you use it.

The same goes for our devices. How we arrange them determines how we will use them, so we should think about this before we organise them.

Look carefully at the way you have organised your own device. What would you say is important to you? Do you have a mass of social media apps front and centre on your homescreen? If so, this would make it very easy to zombie scroll in those in-between moments.

Try shifting the apps you often use to zombie scroll away from your home screen, or remove them altogether so that you need to go online and log in to your account.

What have you decorated your lockscreen with? Does it have a photo of a loved one? If so, this may be adding to the sense of emotional comfort and security you get from your phone. What if you changed that to a photo of a health or life goal? Doing this shifts your phone from a tool of comfort to a tool of motivation. Studying for an exam? If we touch our phone on average over 2600 times a day, then placing the facts, formulas and dates you need to remember on your lockscreen can help you. Make your phone work for YOU.

Maybe you are worried about how much time you spend on a screen. If so, try redesigning it so it looks less appealing. Turn on black-and-white mode on your device. This is something teens often use as a strategy to reduce their screen time – and it works. You could also set a passcode you need to enter every time your phone is locked (and also disable the facial or fingerprint recognition). This will annoy the hell out of you, but will ultimately dissuade you from taking it out every minute or so.

The digital environment we create for ourselves is very important, because we are regularly feeding our brain the content and ideas that lie within it. Problems arise when we haven't created the right environment.

A digital declutter is a bit like a wardrobe clean-out where you evaluate how well your current wardrobe is working for you. Instead of clothes, focus on the digital environment that you have created for yourself.

Look at the apps, programs, websites and uses you are engaging in, and identify those that don't fit anymore, that cause you stress or don't benefit you. Do you only visit shopping sites? Do you have any apps that pull you out of being a consumer and into being a producer – creating, thinking, learning?

You may assess an app's worthiness in terms of how it shapes the way you use your devices. Some apps encourage us to move on when their original purpose is achieved, others are designed to keep us on there, just as YouTube or Netflix auto-play the next video by default. If you've overloaded your devices with too many needy apps, ditch some.

Your ultimate question should be: 'What value does this add to my life?' If you don't have a really good answer, ditch it.

Make it easy to successfully make these changes. Design your devices to help lift you out of the digital habits you want to get rid of.

Be intentional in the way you use your device

There's this incredible study where men and women were given a choice: either be completely alone with your thoughts for 15 minutes or have an electric shock.[36] It seems like an unusual study, but what was even more unusual were the results. Sixty per cent of men and 30 per cent of women actively chose to give themselves an electric shock rather than be deprived of external sensory stimuli.

Our minds are built to engage with the world. They are always scanning, looking for stimuli. That's one of the big reasons we use technology to fill every spare 15 minutes we have.

We are all creatures of habit. It has been said that 'the chains of habit are too light to be felt until they are too heavy to remove'. I don't believe there are necessarily good habits or bad habits, only those that play into your goals and those that don't. Being on our devices purely because we have some time to fill is one of the habits we have with technology that is very unlikely to help us achieve anything that we want to achieve.

Remember, if what you're doing doesn't have a real purpose, ask yourself what gap you are trying to fill, or what stress you are escaping. We need to be honest with ourselves, then take real steps to address our concerns. I can't fix the stress, but I can help you become aware of how you are using your technology to deal with it.

A value-add reason to use technology means not only using it to help you in the functional aspects of your life, but also in helping you grow as a person. One of the brilliant things about technology is that it offers us so many resources, and so many ways to learn and develop ourselves.

I personally use social media to learn. One thing I love to do is follow street artists from around the globe on Instagram. Their photos give me an 'insider', off-the-beaten-track glimpse into the world and other cultures. My dad is a professional photographer, so the beauty of a well-taken photo is something that has been entrenched in me from an early age. From these Instagram artists I learn new photographic techniques, and they give me inspiration for taking better photos when I travel. It's not only about the nice pictures, though. It also reminds me that the world is much larger than our national news cycle. I find it comforting and grounding to be reminded of this regularly.

Some everyday examples of meaningful use:

'I have a fitness app and then a calorie counter thing. They help me understand myself better. Using both together I think is more meaningful and worth my while than just looking at Facebook.'

'My dictionary app is the only app I pay for. I like to learn the word of the day and use it immediately, either in a text, comment, note, or aloud to myself. If I have a minute, I can scroll Instagram or learn the definition of a cool word. A deeper vocabulary will make you a deeper person.'

'To me there's a difference between mindlessly scrolling, and reading a bookmarked article, which is active and intentional. I use a bookmarking tool and learn on the go. Don't leave learning up to chance.'

'I play chess against a computer on my phone if I have 7–10 minutes. Chess builds your problem-solving abilities and strategic thinking, unlike tapping a heart on Instagram.'

'Instead of just a "like", I now always write a comment on social media. I often now get comments back, too. It feels better, like I'm actually doing something meaningful.'

'I listen to podcasts. Podcasts are like eavesdropping on two smart people having a really good conversation. They're great for learning and self-augmentation. After a LinkedIn binge, I feel frazzled. But after a few minutes of a good podcast, I feel inspired and motivated. And they're mostly free.'

'I use YouTube, an app, or any online site to learn something I've always wanted to learn. Yesterday I learnt the best way to BBQ steak. Today was how to wax my car. Sometimes I do this just to get started or sometimes I use it to help me learn it in its entirety.'

'I choose new entertainment options for myself that I usually wouldn't do. I try to aim for something creative, like a new cooking app, yoga, daily ten minutes of meditation, or how to decorate my loungeroom in "beach style". Entertainment isn't only sitting and watching Netflix.'

'I keep a journal on my device. I use my voice recorder to create an audio journal, images, texts. The psychological benefits of journaling are well documented. The best part is that it doesn't even take 15 minutes.'

Take action: plan your escape

When it comes to the choices we make with technology, it can be easy to forget the positives.

For example, we worry that the comparisons that happen on social media impact teenagers' mental health. However, studies show that when teenagers use social media in more creative and interest-driven ways – such as searching for new information or learning new skills about hobbies or things they're interested in – this actually has a positive effect on their sense of achievement, their schoolwork and their overall wellbeing.[37]

What drains us is when we use technology as a crutch to help us through low periods. This is a massive problem, and one we will explore in later chapters. But as always, it is not black and white.

Often when we are stressed or feel like everything in life is going haywire, our automatic response is to sit on our phone and escape. But, with the right skills and know-how, we can ensure this isn't an ongoing problem.

If you tend to escape into your technology when you are feeling stressed, here's a tip: creative content will help you move out of negativity more quickly than meaningless content will.

A study in the *Journal of Positive Psychology* showed that engaging in a creative activity just once a day leads to a more positive state of mind.[38] In this study, 658 adults documented how much time they spent on creative endeavours every day, as well as the positive and negative emotional changes they felt. Over the two weeks there was an upward spiral for wellbeing and creativity in those individuals who engaged in daily creative pastimes.

The participants felt increasingly energetic, enthusiastic and excited each day, as well as feeling more calm, content and relaxed. The boost not only happened on the day the pastime was engaged in, but cumulatively in the days that followed. These people reported feeling happier in their social relationships and at work.

If we use technology to let off steam, ditching the social media scroll and doing something creative to meaningfully and successfully buffer against negative emotions will help us 'feel better'. It will also positively impact other aspects of our lives for days after.

Using technology creatively might mean curating a Pinterest board, writing a product review, or playing an online musical instrument – in other words, activities that almost anyone can do. These digital activities can give us opportunities that time, space, cost or life just haven't allowed us. You may not have a space for a garden at home, or have time to tend to it, but you can express this interest by creating an online garden.

One idea is to create a yearbook for yourself. Snap photos of things that have meant a lot to you over the year and add them to a yearbook album in your photos. You might include a photo of a report that was a huge success at work, or a photo of a ticket stub from a concert you loved. It can focus on life in general or a goal you are working towards. Adding to this, and scrolling through it in those in-between moments, is meaningful, feel-good use of your technology.

Look through your apps and see how many of them are creative. If you don't have any, then get some. Put these apps in an easy-to-access space on your screen, and learn how to use them before those high-stress moments.

Digital fulfilment means using technology in ways that focus on thinking, care, good and community. Express yourself in a way you enjoy on a regular basis, just once a day, and you'll benefit from a more positive state of mind.

Chapter 4

Digital stressors

Technology makes us very,
very busy, and we don't often
step back to consider which
uses are causing us stress.
Now we have the foundation
for using technology well,
we're going to deep dive
into identifying which
technology use causes us
the most stress.

I want you to imagine you're watching a video of a group of people using their phone, tablet or laptop in their usual everyday ways. They're checking Instagram to get their mind off that stressful work project, slipping their phone under their pillow before going to sleep, scrolling mindlessly while waiting at the bus stop.

Not only can you see what they're doing, you can also see how it's making them – and others – feel. Their smile when they send a cheeky text, their exhaustion after sending a pile of work emails, their frustration every time they read that same person's social media post, and the look on their partner's face when they take a quick break from sex to check a new notification.

Stress is one of the main sources of wear and tear on both our minds and our bodies. You are probably familiar with the physical symptoms of high-level stress, such as headaches, sweaty palms, butterflies in the tummy or a racing heart. Our technology use causes us ongoing low-grade stress. The chemicals produced by our body during low-grade stress are the same as those that occur during high-level stress, but the negative effects don't appear immediately. Instead, they occur on a cellular level and eat away at us slowly.

Sounds terrible, right? So let's think about it, so we can change it. Let's consider the key technology stressors that are packing a punch because they occur simultaneously, every day, and across all aspects of our life – when we are at work, at home, with our kids, with our partner and alone.

Unrelenting disruption

Unlike any other object humans have fashioned and owned, technology is not inanimate or passive – it engages with us.

In the early days, we used devices simply to address our needs – to look something up or to contact someone. While we still use them for these things, our devices now open a floodgate of people, groups, businesses and entities who interact with us directly, wherever and whenever we happen to be. This is an unprecedented situation.

Though humans have evolved to be social – this is a key feature of our success as a species – the social structures in which we thrive tend to contain about 150 individuals. The number of smartphone users worldwide means that we now carry around 2 billion potential connections in our pockets every day.[39]

Our peaceful, personal space has now become akin to a crowded online marketplace, and we carry these immense social environments in our pockets through every waking moment of our days.

Controlling who and what enters our world via technology is near impossible, and we are paying a significant mental and physical cost as a result.

Take the work of physicians and the impact digital disruption is having on them. A whopping 26 per cent of physicians have experienced burnout due to the overwhelming amount of online paperwork now required for treating patients.[40] Doctors now spend up to two hours completing online paperwork for every hour of consultation with a patient.[41] This doesn't always fit into their patient schedule, so many doctors spend dozens of hours a week working at home after the kids are in bed, just to keep the digital beast at bay. Doctors with insufficient time to fill in these records at work are 2.8 times more likely to suffer from burnout than those who do.

Many of us can relate to the overwhelming burden of online paperwork and forms. It's in our jobs and also across many aspects of life outside of work.

I worked in a university for many years, and much of my day involved filling in online forms about the work I was going to do, the work I had done, my work plans for next week, next month. Online paperwork about my work massively ate into the time I had to actually do my work.

Even those of us who think we are in good shape when it comes to digital distraction often have our device near us when we are doing something that's not related to technology. We may be reading a print copy of a book, yet have a device near us with multiple tabs open. Notifications are probably popping up right now.

One client who likes to keep up to date with the news told me, 'I leave my news apps open all day. The problem is that they constantly bombard me with notifications, so I find myself simultaneously worried about many political issues and also distracted.'

One of the biggest issues with digital disruptions is that it feels like we have only wasted a few seconds. Glancing at our email in the middle of cooking dinner, or quickly checking our messages while talking to the kids seems relatively innocent.

Some people suggest that we have taken multitasking to new heights. But we're not actually multitasking. We are switching rapidly between different activities, and the problem is, our brain is not designed to do this.

Do any of the following apply to your behaviour at work?

'I keep my phone out in the open, where I can see it.'

'I keep my inbox and messages open all day to ensure I don't miss notifications.'

'When having a long chat with someone, I often look at my screen either during the conversation or directly after it.'

'I find myself checking my work emails mid-gym session, mid-supermarket shopping, mid-car drive, mid-gardening, mid-anything.'

Let's look at the impact of digital disruption. It's 4 pm, we're bored at work and check a notification that's come through. Say it's from a shop we subscribed to three years ago. We look at the jeans they have on sale, but after some deliberation decide we don't really need new jeans. After we finish reading the message, we get back to our task.

Here's the stinger: it takes us an average of 23 minutes and 15 seconds to recover from the distraction and be fully on task again.[42]

Do all digital distractions have the same effect? Absolutely not. We treat each digital distraction differently. Some we bin straight away, and others we give much more attention to. However, every notification, every article and every social media check requires us to shift our focus and to make a decision on it. Those seemingly small interruptions can really add up, dramatically affecting our productivity.

Staggeringly, the latest research shows that we now spend an average of just 90 minutes in total during each workday thinking and working deeply. To compensate for these constant interruptions we work faster, and often more superficially.

Sounds like an effective solution, right? But it has a cost, and the impact hits us all in different ways.

It takes time away from quality decisions and effective communication.

> It leads to a sense of overwhelm; we feel like we are doing twice the amount of work, but in the same amount of time and for the same amount of money.

In the short term, we adapt well to these demands, but in the long term the stress hormones adrenaline and cortisol create a physiological hyper-alert state. This means that we are always scanning for stimuli, provoking a sense of addictive-type behaviours, which we temporarily soothe by 'checking in' on Facebook.

And it's not just our work that is suffering. All these notifications can make us feel like we have lost control, and without control we feel powerless to pursue what we value. This affects our sense of achievement, which in turn brings us close to burnout. A whopping 85 per cent of us say we feel physically and emotionally drained from so many disruptions, and experience more stress, higher frustration and more time pressure because we feel like we can never catch up in all aspects of our lives.

The only person who truly knows the impact digital disturbance has on us, is us. The only way that we can understand its impact is if we join the dots for ourselves. Awareness, my friend, is an incredibly powerful first step.

Contactable me

Which of these two statements do you think is the most correct?

a) Everyone's lives are incredibly busy, so we need to make sure people can always reach us via technology.

b) Always being available via our devices means that our lives have become incredibly busy.

It's hard to choose, as they are both correct. Our 'always available' culture has been dressed up as the answer to our time-poor lives, but it's also hurting us.

Picture this scenario. It's 7 am, and *ping!* Your boss has 'just one quick question'.

Then *ping!* The plumber needs to arrange a visit.

Ping! A funny YouTube video is sent on a group chat.

Ping! Uncle Pete wants to know when you'll be dropping in.

Ping! Your parcel will be delivered today.

Ping! Your parcel has been delivered.

Ping! Rate how well we did delivering your parcel.

We are overwhelmed by social contact, and we've had to change our communication style in order to keep up.

Humans have always been social beings. But remember those long chats we might have had with friends over the phone or in person? Many of these have been replaced with quick automated responses, like emojis and automated replies. These make it much easier to stay connected with everyone in our life, but the ways we connect are becoming increasingly impersonal.

> Friendships are being reduced to 'keeping up'. The intimacy and deep social connection that we as humans need is subsequently eroding away.

One of my clients told me that when communicating with friends and family online, she'd begun to feel like she was performing for the makers of the social media platform, rather than having real conversations with people who mattered to her. She had three Twitter accounts, a Facebook and an Instagram account, and was on about a dozen Slack teams for business communication. She felt that there were too many channels running concurrently, and it was getting too hard to keep up. 'I feel unfocused all the time,' she said.

Limiting friends on Facebook to people we know well doesn't make much difference. Neither does bunching together a whole lot of social networking apps to relieve our social disconnectedness. Our digital stress is not about numbers. It's about why we do what we do on our devices.

We seem to have fallen into the belief that every inquiry, message and email has to be answered right away. Many of us will interrupt an in-person conversation to attend to an online notification. Remember, 10 per cent of us will check a notification during sex.

Why do we feel this need to jump to attention?

We feel like we have a social obligation to rapidly respond to notifications. We stare at those little bubbles while awaiting an incoming text message, and feel pressured to like, retweet or favourite a post as soon as we can.

The digital dream was that technology would allow us to work remotely and flexibly. If we believe recent

Nobody asked us to be rapid notification responders. We just fell into this learned behaviour, and got used to being on the scene as soon as something happens.

headlines, that transition is all too easy. But the reality is that we've turned our whole life into our workplace. First, we took 'extra' work home to do at night. That progressed to regularly logging into work email from home. Then we downloaded the app to make checking work email quicker and easier.

Digital convenience is very seductive. It can save us time and uplift us. But although these small conveniences have been efficient, they incrementally bring us down and disempower us.

Cortisol is produced when we are under stress. Its role is to keep the body on high alert, by increasing blood sugar levels and suppressing the immune system. This serves us well when dealing with an immediate physical threat. But when we are faced with ongoing emotional stressors (like 24/7 work emails), chronically elevated cortisol levels can lead to all sorts of health problems, including diabetes, obesity, high blood pressure and depression. The long-term risks for disease, heart attack, stroke and dementia are also increased. 'Burnout' has now been classified as a health condition by the World Health Organization, and it is translating into increased cognitive load and reduced employee performance – nullifying the purpose of increasing digital connectivity in the first place!

The stress caused by our technology use has crept up on us. As our devices have become more advanced, we have adapted by making small changes in the ways we use them. It's exactly why a big part of living well with technology is about being mindful of what kind of stress we feel and why.

Information overload

Every time we go online we are inundated with words, pictures, videos, comments, opinions, information, advertising, conspiracy theories; the list goes on. To stand out in this crowded space, online content is increasingly designed to pierce our vulnerabilities – to make us shocked, scared, surprised, excited. It's all about getting a reaction. 'Information overload' is the side effect of the quantity and design of online content.

The coronavirus pandemic led to massive information overload, making it difficult to separate fact from fiction. For example, 'panic buying' got excessive airplay on social media and in 24/7 news cycles. For weeks, we were bombarded with content about tensions at the supermarkets. Some of it was factual, but some was blatantly untrue or exaggerated in the hope of getting noticed.

Humans have this remarkable ability to both 'know' and 'not know' at the same time. Collectively, this coverage whipped up a sense of panic, and people began to stockpile – toilet paper, flour, rice, cake mix, hand sanitiser – even though many reputable news sites were saying that there was no scarcity of these products.

Remember, anxiety and fear affect decision-making. The panic buying was not us dealing with Covid-19 as a health condition, it was how we asserted control in the face of the fearful and extreme content we were encountering.

Much of the stress that technology causes us is because of the way information and content is designed and delivered. Information overload is an old problem; research on its effects dates back to the 1960s. However, the problem has been magnified by digital innovation. We are contending with an 'information avalanche' – an overwhelming volume of information that flows relentlessly. This avalanche impedes our information processing ability. There is way too much content for us to view, let alone synthesise.

The internet has made amazing progress in eliminating ignorance, but also in perpetuating it.

We access so much information, but often we are not particularly observant, leaving us with just an impression or a feeling about what we've been looking at.

An equally stressful factor is that we are now inundated with false news and misinformation online. Why? Because it travels faster than real news – often much, much faster. It's designed to grab our attention by connecting with our more extreme emotions. We get caught up in the moment and retweet a terrifying headline before even reading the accompanying article. The overwhelming emotional content creates inconsistency in our decision-making. It's a bit like being hit in the head with every terrifying or shocking post we see – it impacts us both physically and mentally.

The kind of information we grapple with online is not likely to change anytime soon. We've stopped paying for news, algorithms are feeding us more stuff that's like the last thing we clicked on, and news has begun to be 'created', not reported. Plus, outrage and fear is profitable.

I often imagine a toolkit that I carry with me every day containing the tools I need to improve my overall digital lifestyle. For me, being able to objectively consider the information I'm reading or seeing online is crucial. We don't want to become obsessed with questioning absolutely everything, because this can lead to becoming cynical, rather than critical, but it's important to know that authoritative and credible sources are out there. We can take matters into our own hands by proactively evaluating content.

Losing control

The common theme between these major stressors is loss of control. We may not be able to control all aspects of our technology life, but we do get to control our impulses and our skills. And this is incredibly powerful.

Knowing how to use technology in a stress-free way is not something that is coming naturally to us. And why should it? As humans, we've never had to manage a phenomenon like technology before. We've adjusted and fashioned ways of handling the seemingly infinite and magical resources it offers, but the habits we've formed have sent our lives out of kilter. As a result, our technology use is causing us a lot more pain than pleasure. We can't live our entire lives this way – if we do, we'll never actually live our own lives.

Take action: 'untrouble' your notifications

One of the things that worries us about our technology use is how many times a day we pick up our devices. Our notifications are often compared to a slot machine and the tactics these machines use to keep us gambling.

Let's think about this analogy some more. It may feel like we have no control over wanting to check our notifications, yet most of us can easily stroll by a slot machine without wanting to play it. Sure, they may use similar tactics, but they don't have the same effect on us.

What is it that alerts you to your notifications (perhaps it is the *ping!* you get) and what is it that makes you want to open them? It's different for each of us, so there are different remedies.

It can be helpful to separate the notifications we get. You can assign a different sound for every type of notification. A bell sound for Messenger, a popcorn sound for a text, a twinkle for your emails, and no sound at all for others. Categorising notifications in this way helps you prioritise them. If you want to stay in touch with the kids, maybe ensure you always look at texts, but ignore emails and Messenger until later.

Batching apps by purpose or importance also helps to separate them. We can group our apps by theme, such as dating, friends, work, entertainment, communication and so on. Managing the apps in groups means we can then turn them off depending on their priority. For example, we can turn off notifications for work apps on the weekend, or turn off the social apps during the 9–5 workday. This helps us to concentrate on one activity and tune out the rest.

Some people feel guilty about the idea of not responding to notifications straight away, worried that others will feel ignored. If this is a concern, let others know what to expect from you.

It helps to remember that social media is a business, and these platforms aim to get as much of our attention as possible.

It's like dieting – you need to set boundaries. The support of others, particularly at the beginning stages, will help you stick to those boundaries.

Be critical of what technology companies are doing to keep us coming back. Developers know too well that the apps we put on our homescreen tend to consume the majority of our time, leaving other installed apps on the margins. Apps also lose 80 per cent of their audience within the first three days of being installed.[43] This is why developers have designed notifications encouraging users to open and use their app. They are always looking for ways to drive up use of THEIR app in a highly competitive market.

That's right, it's *their* app – it's not about us, it's about getting more usage of their product. That manipulation is a powerful motivator for me to not give in to them.

Chapter 5

Digital interactions

We can't blame technology for relationships gone wrong. The impulse to disappear from an unsatisfying connection has probably existed since Cro-Magnon met Neanderthal. However, the way others interact with us online for work, pleasure, play and love has become increasingly confusing, complex and reactionary.

Tim: 'Oh, he soft-ghosted you.'

Brad: 'What does that mean?'

Tim: 'It's when they acknowledge your message by simply "liking" it or adding an emoji. Technically, they were the last person to interact, but you risk double texting if you say anything after that. It's checkmate.'

Ghosting in all its forms is one of the most prolific and unpleasant communication trends of our time.

> Our sense of right and wrong shapes our daily interactions, but people will do and say things online that they would never do in real life.

In real life we clam up; online we wear our hearts on our sleeves. We become bolder and less afraid to speak our mind.

There is an increasing dark undertone to our digital communication. More than one in three of us have personally been affected by toxic online behaviour or encounters that aim to vent, attack, offend, bully and shame. These actions are harmful and this behaviour needs to stop, full stop. Sadly, the behaviour has become so pervasive that a whole host of terms have emerged to describe it, hence you'll find a new glossary throughout this chapter.

It is important to be aware of the effect toxic online behaviour has on us. Being conscious of how and why technology is used by others makes us better able to minimise the stress it can cause.

The social contract

Most of the digital issues we are experiencing – the bad habits we have formed, and the wiped-out, exhausted feeling we get from technology use – centre around platforms where we come together socially, such as social media, video games, comments sections and dating apps.

Like pretty much all the online platforms we use, the founders of these platforms say that they didn't know how their platform was going to be used when they created it.

The founders of Twitter openly say that they had no idea what they were creating. Similarly, Kevin Systrom, co-creator of Instagram, said in an interview that Instagram was designed as a fun, creative tool for photographers and designers to use. Very quickly, people outside that community started using it to display their lives. Accounts were (and still are) public by default, which meant that if you were willing to share your life, people would follow you. As a result, we have seen an increase in social comparison and jealousy.

Twitter co-founder Jack Dorsey stated:

'We thought if we gave everyone a voice, that life would be instantly better. Then after the 2016 USA election when one of the candidates used it very loud and boisterously, we have to look again at how social media can either create divisions or also create unity.'[52]

We often blame the billionaire thirty-somethings in Silicon Valley who invented these platforms for creating something that's causing us substantial harm, and of course they cannot be let off scot-free. However, it's important to remember that there is not one single online platform or device that is pure good. As users, we need to learn how to emphasise the good and manage the bad.

One of the most astounding things about social media is that it genuinely amplifies the human condition. It taps into our need to connect with people and ideas. That can be a good thing, and it's why many of us are drawn to it. However, it also holds a massive magnifying glass up to our vulnerabilities: envy, insecurity, loneliness, anger. These vulnerabilities are not new, but our use of social media brings them out.

A study by the UK Royal Society for public health policy stated that 'Instagram was found to have the most overall negative impact on young people's mental health. It negatively impacts body image and sleep. It increases bullying and FOMO. And leads to greater feelings of anxiety, depression, and loneliness.'[44]

But it's not just Instagram, it's all social platforms. And it's not only a teenager's problem. Whether you're 16, 24 or 45, the potential for harm is the same.

Judgements and pile-ons

It's not uncommon to unlock our device and step straight into an angry Twitter rant about the government, toxic comments on a news item about race or religion,[45] or the public shredding of a person's integrity. Do not think for a moment that this is all water off a duck's back to us.

On average, we spend between two and four hours on social media per day, and our brains are sponges, absorbing and internalising everything we're taking in.

YouTube megastar James Charles lost 3 million subscribers in a matter of days when his followers decided the star's admittedly brattish and ungrateful remarks were poor form. He became yet another victim of 'cancel culture' and the unprecedented level of co-ordinated anger and aggression we are starting to see online.

Public online shaming can happen to anyone. There was the university professor whom amateur internet detectives wrongly described as a white supremacist on social media. More than 11,000 people retweeted his photo to publicly shame him.

His home address was published on social media and he endured angry demands that he be stripped of his job.

Then there was the web developer whose off-colour comments on social media about 'big dongles' lost him his job – and led to a Twitter evisceration of the woman who 'outed' him. Or the 21-year-old student whose 17-second video posing in front of a boarded-up store during the #blacklivesmatter protests was viewed over 29 million times, prompting an extreme backlash.

The internet has made it easier for people to be called out for behaviour that really isn't okay, and that they would once have gotten away with. But it has also led to angry mobs whipping up a frenzy of hatred, often giving little pause to consider the facts.

Some people strategically use moral grandstanding to enhance their social rank.[46] In days gone by, if you were targeted by an angry mob, you could physically remove yourself and start over. But you can't leave the internet, whether your involvement was your mistake or someone else's.

Like almost every aspect of our digital lives, this negativity was not what we planned for the internet. The hostility started happening, and then it grew.

The thing about toxic online behaviour is that it centres on social rejection. Slip-ups are not tolerated online, and there are never-ending rants about how crap everyone and everything is.

> While the toxicity may not be directed at us personally, we don't always realise how ragged we become from constantly being immersed in it.

Long periods of negativity have detrimental effects on our mental, emotional and physical health. The hate we see online lowers our mood and drains us of energy, leaving us fatigued. It's like that dull headache that's been humming in your head for weeks. All of a sudden it starts to roar.

Darker terms for our digital dictionary:

Cancel culture: co-ordinated anger and aggression towards a person online with the aim of cancelling them

Clickjacking: using a fake weblink to trick users into revealing personal information

Cyber flashing: sending explicit images anonymously – usually via AirDrop or Bluetooth – to strangers in public places

Dark patterns: tricks and manipulations that online companies build into their sites and apps to mislead or confuse us

Flaming: hurling insults at other players in a video game because you're losing

Griefing: deliberately irritating and harassing other players in a video game

A little bit louder now

One of the best things about the internet is that it gives us all a voice. There is no other platform that allows everyone to have their say to such a big audience whenever they want. This means the internet can be a great equaliser, giving voice to those who are marginalised.

It can also be used to advance a social cause – this is known as 'clicktivism' or 'hashtag activism'. #metoo and #blacklivesmatter are great examples of how technology can help to spread and amplify a movement, although the jury is still out on how much engagement this sort of activism actually creates. Simple acts such as sharing a post can make people feel like they have done their bit, and so stop them from taking further action.

But the negative, angry and opportunistic side of the internet can also make it the great unequaliser.

Unfortunately, while some toxic behaviour online is unintentional, treating others badly online has become a deliberate act. This behaviour often preys on people's fears, as shocking content is more likely to be shared.

Children are an obvious point of vulnerability for parents. Online hoaxes that threaten children's safety often go viral as parents frantically try to protect their own and other children.

Take the MOMO hoax. The message was that if your child saw the ghoulish MOMO image online, the figure would encourage the child to kill themselves. The image was said to be found all over YouTube. Children aged 4–15 years watch YouTube for an average of 85 minutes every day, so the chances of them seeing this image was terrifyingly high.[47]

Toxic online behaviour loves the surprise element. When confronted with surprising new information, humans don't always respond logically. Our brains are set up to give us easy answers. So if there's a hoax that appeals to people's emotions or intuition, it's going to trick them. Unsurprisingly, MOMO led to a worldwide effort by parents, traditional media, police and schools, all frantic to protect kids. Eventually, MOMO was found to be a hoax and disappeared as fast as it had spread.

Twitter co-founder Jack Dorsey disclosed that the worst things to happen on his platform were doxxing and violent threats. He also pointed out the deception of content on Twitter that 'misleads people into off-platform actions'. An example of this was a scam where users were sent off Twitter to a fake site where they texted a number under the pretence that they will be registered to vote.

A major issue is that there is little reputational or punitive risk involved with bad behaviour online – including from the administrators of big sites like Twitter. Online social spaces are not regulated by laws and cooperation in the same way as life offline. So long as posts don't cross the line into what the platforms define as 'hate speech' or what a particular company defines as 'harassment', there is little users can do. Unfortunately, this is unlikely to be resolved any time soon.

A player might get sent off the field in a real-life sporting game for 'flaming', or 'griefing' (deliberately irritating and harassing other players), but there is no such consequence in online video-game play. As a result, kids growing up today are learning that 'bad behaviour' online is tolerated, even expected. This can affect the way they behave offline as well.

And it's not just about rules and regulations.

When you criticise someone online, you don't get the visible cues that you're hurting their feelings.

You don't see their body language – the bow of their head, the furrow of their brow, that wounded look in their eyes. The tone of voice of the person being criticised is also missing online. Studies suggest that a lack of eye contact is a more potent driver of hostility than being anonymous and invisible.

The internet also hides the aggressor – the one dishing out the hurt. If you've ever been 'cyber-flashed' you'll know what I mean. Cyber flashing involves explicit images being anonymously sent – usually via AirDrop or Bluetooth – to strangers in public places. Imagine you're a 13-year-old girl catching the train home from school, and all of a sudden a sexually explicit image appears on your phone. The image can't be traced, meaning the perpetrator can simply sit there and enjoy the victim's reaction. Like other online bullying, cyber flashing aims to shock, and to make you feel vulnerable.

It's also easy to hide in the anonymity of a comments section, posting derogatory or discriminatory comments without fear of repercussions. Verbally abusing other players in a video game is easy when you're using a pseudonym.

Unfortunately, if someone is having a bad day – or a bad life – the internet makes it easy for them to lash

Have you encountered these terms?

Ghosting: stopping all communication with someone online without any warning or justification

Hivemind: the expectation to conform to popular opinion online or risk being the target of hate

Lynching: a co-ordinated social media celebrity hate storm

Soft-ghosting: the same as ghosting, but with a thin veil of nicety, such as liking someone's online post and then stopping all communication without any warning or justification

Troll farming: employing real people to flood the internet with comments supporting a particular viewpoint; also known as 'astroturfing'

out more frequently or intensely than they would in person. It's called the 'toxic inhibition' effect.

And now, thanks to the way we've developed algorithms, people might even pay more attention to these posts. Online content that expresses outrage is 20 per cent more likely to be shared on social media feeds than content that doesn't.[48] The result is an ecosystem that selects for us the most outrageous content, paired with a platform that makes it easier than ever to express outrage. These elements make it open season for bad behaviour. Not everyone will take the opportunity to act this way, but those who do stand out.

Textual chemistry

Toxic behaviour and divisive language on the internet can affect us whether we directly engage with it or not, but it's an even heavier burden to bear when the anger and dissatisfaction targets us personally. This pierces some of the very elements that make us human: our desires, anxieties and fears.

Forty-three per cent of 25–34-year-olds and 25 per cent of 35–44-year-olds use dating apps.[49] 'Textual chemistry' can be a huge benefit of this new platform for connection, but textual toxicity has also become commonplace.

Take this online dating situation. Recently, Jen matched with a man on Tinder who invited her over to his house at 11 pm. After she declined, he called her 83 times between 1 am and 5 am.

When she finally answered and asked him to stop, he said, 'You would have been just one screw because you're an ugly fat bitch.' He ended the exchange with a message: 'Cya you disgusting, fat, time-wasting whore'.

Although it was scary, Jen wasn't shocked, as she'd had plenty of exchanges with men who had 'suppressed anger' about their lack of success on the dating market. 'At a certain point,' she said, 'it becomes exhausting to keep putting yourself out there and to receive so little back.'

Does this happen often on dating apps? Yes.

Is it easy to shrug off a comment like 'disgusting fat pig' as idiotic spite? Yes.

Is it easy to forget this person and move on to the next gal/guy on the app? Yes.

Would I ever say that this doesn't affect us? HELL NO.

Jen fobbed off this toxic encounter with what seems like a casual 'Shit happens' attitude. She even justified his actions, saying it must be frustrating if he's not having any luck with online dating, and alludes to the idea that she, along with all the other women who turned him down, are to blame.

Jen's acceptance of this behaviour makes it clear that this is not a one-off situation for her. However, her justification also suggests that we should expect to be treated in this way when dating online. Many of us do this – we shrug it off, or think we can shrug it off.

The way we communicate with ourselves is more important than you think. Dismissing something as a #badhookup or #onlinedatinglife does not take into account the way it makes us feel or the stress that it causes.

Let's call this behaviour what it really is: someone taking their problems out on someone else. By making someone else feel bad, they make themselves feel better. And what's worse, these cowards are doing this behind the anonymous shield of the internet.

Many people justify this as 'to be expected', given the marketplace vibe of dating apps. We can pull out our device and 'shop' hundreds and thousands of potential new dates who are all just a few swipes away. Most people now aspire to date someone who is 25 per cent more desirable than themselves, suggesting we're pickier than we used to be.[50]

Research consistently shows that the screen mediates our sense of agency. It makes us braver and bolder, and more likely to do and say what we really think. Asking someone for a date or a hook-up behind the protection of a screen is less scary than doing so in person. Ask enough people, and someone is bound to say yes.

The abundance of people online makes us quicker to discard a relationship, because finding is 'easy'. It's supply and demand 101: 'if this relationship doesn't go well, there are 20 other people just like you in my inbox'. The problem is that this has made toxic behaviour more commonplace, affecting both our stress and our mental health.

I'm not saying you should avoid online dating. Where you meet and date is not important, but how we communicate with each other is. Do not kid yourself that someone else writing nasty comments to you via a dating app – or any other online communication platform – doesn't affect you.

Everybody hurts

The fact is, whether it happens online or offline, rejection and anger hurt. We never become desensitised to it. We are human.

Part of the pain we feel is that because the person causing the hurt is hidden online, there's little opportunity for resolution. It's like walking through a haunted house. You can't see who's scaring you, and you don't know what's around the corner. Flick the light on, however, and it's not so scary.

Imagine you gathered all the people who have trolled you, ghosted you or directed nasty online comments at you into a room. How would this help you to resolve the pain they caused you?

You now have a chance to find out who they are, their vulnerabilities, why they sent the messages, which would help resolve the internal conflict you feel. Seeing and meeting you could also cause the offenders to feel responsibility for their actions – a change in trajectory for both parties.

We often worry about the ways teenagers communicate online and the effect this has on their mental and emotional wellbeing, but we also need to look after ourselves. Whether it's romantic partners, video game opponents, clients, friends, family members or work colleagues, when people use the online space to trash talk in ways that target our insecurities, this can eat away at our self-esteem, and nurture the negative views we have of ourselves.

The impact of this on us is like rust on metal. The more it happens, the more it eats away. It can lead to a habit of comparing yourself to others, playing the victim, negative self-talk, and more.

It's a common misconception that online complaints, anger and harassment are just a fact of life now – or worse, that dishing it out is an integral part of enjoying a video game or engaging with the news on social media. It's not.

We tell ourselves, 'Don't worry, it's just Twitter, it doesn't matter.' It matters.

We lull ourselves into a false sense of security by thinking that the 'online' aspect of toxic behaviour acts like a shield, protecting us from the damage and stress it could cause. It doesn't.

What happens online impacts all aspects of our life. Our online and offline lives are no longer separate.

Tone deaf

Online communication also causes confusion because of the limitations of online communication.

If you've ever had anyone misinterpret your text you'll know that part of the issue relates to the challenges of relying on written text to communicate. It's like telling two people who are having a face-to-face conversation to put on a blindfold and earmuffs. They can't see or hear the other person, and must guess what the other is trying to say just from words they read on a phone screen.

When communicating via text, email and social media posts, tone, intention and body language can be lost. Even in telephone conversations we have a vocal reference to fall back on to prevent misunderstanding. Nothing prepared us as a civilisation to discuss romantic, financial, emotional, legal and potential life and death conversations without any of those cues.

If people send a video, images, memes, links, emojis or reactions with a message, these can all be interpreted in multiple ways, with constantly changing meanings.

If an ex sent you a message with a gun emoji and no text, how should you interpret that? In a case in France, the court decided that this 'amounted to a death threat', and consequently, the man who did so was sentenced to six months' imprisonment.[51]

The reality is, if we're looking to reduce the emotional and mental tension and issues that technology is causing, it makes sense to consider how our online communications are making us feel.

A tip here is to control your feed and who and what you let into your life. Don't accept being treated badly online.

We are a combination of our habits, behaviours, choices and past conditioning. Negativity in online communication is certainly not an easy problem to solve, but neither is it an inevitability we have to live with. We can't keep this from happening to us, but we can get better at taking action to make sure that our online interactions do not burden or stress us.

Unsubscribe and unfollow content that doesn't make you feel good, or that doesn't offer anything of value to you. Putting up with unwanted content should not be the price of using the internet.

Too often we get stuck in a particular mindset and create and recreate routines that can lead to harmful thoughts and behaviours. If we accept being treated badly as 'normal', the resultant stress does not stop once we close our laptop. It carries into our day, and into other aspects of our life.

We all need a feel-good, feel-bad meter that shows us the content we actually engage with online and where that content is damaging us. Is there much range in the people and topics that we engage with, the kinds of accounts we follow, the purpose of the content we consume? How siloed are the posts and views that actually come our way?

We need to be guiding ourselves and others towards more balanced points of view, more balanced content, and healthier contributions that genuinely help us to learn and grow.

Take action: step out of the hate

It's important to work out what we want from the online platforms we use. It's a bit like a work environment. The tasks we complete at work contribute to the meaning and satisfaction we gain from our job, and to how happy it makes us. But equally important to our sense of meaning is our environment: our workmates, lunchtime chats, the sense of fun and camaraderie.

The same can be said for our digital lives. We want to immerse ourselves in an online atmosphere that is positive, enlivening and has meaning for us.

A study of the 777 million Facebook posts uploaded in 2018, which I'm sure many of us contributed to, showed that the 500 most popular posts were inspirational, funny or practical.[53] In other words, they were 'feel-good' in nature. These are the kinds of messages that are genuinely spreading on social media because they give us meaning. It's up to us to be a part of that, rather than being part of the problem.

We tend to live in our own little bubbles on social media. But if we lock ourselves into one way of looking at the world, we become more vulnerable to extreme views and to being manipulated online.

A 16-year-old boy once showed me a video he'd been watching online. It was footage of a road-rage incident. This video (and the playlist that followed it) subtly communicated the idea that road rage and violence are a normal part of life. Algorithms and personalisation of content mean that future video suggestions for this boy will portray similar aggressive acts. If he keeps watching the suggested videos, and doesn't talk about them with anyone or seek others' opinions, then his ideas will be skewed to thinking that this kind of aggressive behaviour is normal and okay.

We want to come away from social media feeling like we've learned something new and beneficial.

We need to think about the content we engage with on social media. Look at the feed that you've curated, and consider what it is actually giving you. A constant rundown of fashion specials will not nurture your growth as a person, nor will it help your stress levels or your mental health.

Step out of the hate, and seek out positivity instead. Break out of doomscrolling. It's easy to angrily scroll Facebook or Twitter, or panic read the news until you're a bundle of anxiety. I've done it. Most of us do. But if we can become aware of how much negativity we are bringing into our world via technology, we can change it.

Share good.

Follow good.

Create good.

Chapter 6

Digital manipulation

Here's a tip: never have sex in front of your home smart speaker. It was recently leaked that employees of some big technology companies have been secretly listening to – and transcribing! – snippets of our private conversations recorded through our home smart speaker or the voice assistant on our smart devices.

Many technology companies have now sheepishly revealed that this was something they considered to be necessary practice in order to improve their products.

At what point did we sign up for eavesdropping?

The technology industry is highly competitive, and the sneaky practices they use to keep the clicks coming show little consideration for how these affect us or what we agree is acceptable.

Maybe we forgot to untick a tiny, almost invisible box on our screen that consents to random people listening to our conversations.

Or maybe we didn't realise that clicking 'OK' meant we were agreeing to being eavesdropped on, as well as granting access to our contacts, messages, browsing activity, photos or location information.

> Technology companies design their products to be as 'sticky' (read: addictive) as possible.

They hire behavioural science experts to develop strategies that exploit our psychology. They trick us into clicking and agreeing when we don't even realise what we are doing.

While we may never be privy to all the tactics online companies use on us, we all feel more in control in environments that we understand. Let's take a look at the ploys the technology industry use to engineer their apps, sites and devices to be as irresistible as possible. This will help us take our power back.

Dark patterns

Imagine for a moment that you are a student. After paying bills and tuition fees you only have $21.25 in your bank account this week. In a week you'll receive your pay from your part-time job as a cashier. You're pretty sure you can manage with only $21 until then.

The next day your bank account has just $6.25 in it. You forgot to cancel your music subscription after your free trial ended. Without warning, you've been charged for the next month.

You're a victim of dark patterns.

While terms like 'dark patterns' and 'deceptive design' may be new to us, we engage with them every day on our screens. These are the tricks and manipulations that companies build into their sites and apps to mislead or confuse us. They're designed to get us to make a purchase or share our data, or to take advantage of us in some other way.

You might say, 'Well, if we forget to unsubscribe, we really can't blame the company for that.' Sure, but that forgetfulness is one of the things that these companies bank on. The trial is *intentionally* designed with the requirement to sign up by handing over our credit card details. An expiry date is *intentionally* included so that conversion can happen quickly. And we get no warning that the free trial is about to end.

It's a trap.

The trap works because our brains are already overloaded with too much information when we're online. Adding more information makes this even worse, which makes it easier for tech companies to trick us into doing exactly what they want us to do.

It's like feeding someone until they are so full they can hardly move. We are digitally stuffed, and that makes us an easy target.

Having too much information to deal with is often referred to as cognitive overload. We feel this overload more acutely when we are doing something that requires us to concentrate, like signing up to a new account or making a purchase online. So placing an 'automatic renew' when we are cognitively overloaded from the sign-up process means that we are distracted, and not thinking as clearly as we usually do. We may not even notice that the auto renew box is already ticked for us. We're even less likely to notice it when another decoy tactic is employed – using small font and placing it away from the main activity that we are concentrating on, or colouring the auto-renew option red instead of green, playing on our assumptions that green is 'agree' and red is 'don't agree'.

Many dark patterns exploit cognitive biases. This means that they tap into our basic desires and instincts.

We tend to remember the decisions that we make as being better than they actually are. We fancy ourselves as good decision-makers, and dark patterns play on this.

Take this standard online shopping 'catch-and-kill':

1. You are browsing for shoes online and add a couple of pairs to your cart, but you're not seriously considering purchasing. A pop-up window appears asking if you'd like to sign up in order to get a discount on your first purchase – you agree. Eventually, however, you decide you don't need the shoes and leave the site without purchasing.

2. While you're browsing another website, a follow-me ad pops up on your screen showing you the same shoes. This works on a key marketing idea that you need to see something multiple times for it to really lodge in your brain.

3. Later that day you get a gentle reminder about the 'two items still in your shopping cart'. This tactic is strategically designed to shift our thinking back to the products that we ourselves selected. You think about the choices that you personally made – they must be good, right? This can often sway us to look at those items again.

4. If you didn't act at step 3 by making a purchase, you'll get this same gentle reminder again in the coming days.

5. The next time you go on that site, your choices will still be in your shopping cart. By now you're sure they're what you want, so you buy them. You get a message, 'Great choice!' immediately after your purchase. This plays to our humanity and confirms that YOU make great decisions.

Watch out!

Dark patterns are found everywhere online, although some of the worst examples are on shopping sites, where profits are directly at stake. A study by researchers at Princeton University and the University of Chicago examined 53,000 product pages on 11,000 shopping websites.[54] One in ten sites were found to use dark patterns to deceive us into spending more money online, like sneaking items into carts before checkout.

Here are some commonly used dark patterns to look out for when you're shopping online, signing up for a new service, or even just spending time on social media – after all, those sites are buying our attention. Hopefully this information will empower you and help you dissect the manipulative content we see on our screens.

Forced continuity
Forced continuity is when we sign up for a 'free trial', and have to give our credit card details. The intention is that we will continue to use the service after the free trial ends. And usually our card is charged without any warning, so we don't get a chance to cancel.

Hidden costs

One of the most common transactions where we encounter hidden costs is when booking a flight. You've found the cheapest ticket, you enter all your details to buy it, and then at the last step you find out that you must pay an additional 'service fee' or 'handling cost'. This usually happens moments before checkout, and we cannot finalise the purchase without agreeing to these additional costs.

This tactic exploits the 'sunk cost fallacy' cognitive bias. This works on the assumption that we will feel so invested in the process by this stage – we've put so much work in to finding the best-price ticket – that we will agree to the additional charges because we don't want to waste our effort.

Sly upselling

Online travel bookings are also notorious for this one, too. Sly upselling is when additional items are automatically added to our basket as we complete our purchase. Often with a travel booking, travel insurance is added to our cart and we have to manually remove it. The automatic inclusion is designed to make us believe we need those extras.

What if you were at the supermarket and the cashier added more items to your trolley without asking, just because they thought you might need them?

Action block

I have been seeing this a lot lately: when something on a website or app is made more difficult than it should be. An example is sites that make it more difficult to decline the cookies user agreement than to accept it. There may only be a big 'accept' button visible, and it's only if you click on the tiny 'learn more' button that a hidden 'decline' button is revealed. Because the decline option is so much harder to find, most users just click accept.

Scarcity bias

Scarcity bias is designed to create a sense of urgency around your purchasing decision. You might receive a pop-up saying '35 people are also viewing this property', '85 per cent of these products are already sold out', 'You have three minutes remaining to make this reservation' or 'Jill from Sydney just bought a 400-litre stainless-steel fridge'. My question is, 'Who is Jill and where is the evidence that she is a real person who made a real purchase?'

This tactic works in two ways. It makes you think that the item is very popular, so you should purchase it too. And it plays on anticipated regret – you don't want to feel disappointment at missing out.

There is no guarantee that these claims are authentic – in fact, in many cases, these numbers are either generated randomly or set to decrease according to a pre-timed schedule. The Princeton and Chicago university study found instances of bogus countdown clocks for expiring deals (refreshing the site would restart the timer) and unsubstantiated claims of low inventory, which pressure us into making choices that benefit the retailer.

Fake reviews

According to Harvard Business School, a one-star increase in a Yelp rating leads to a revenue increase of between 5 and 9 per cent.[55] Online reviews can make or break a business, but between 20 and 40 per cent of online reviews are fake.[56] That's according to research by the University of Illinois and some of the world's best search engine optimisation companies.

Websites often show testimonials with vague origins, and 'review farms' have sprung up, forming a new industry where businesses pay to obtain five-star reviews. You only need to type 'buy reviews' into your search engine to see how extensive the fake review industry is.

Misdirection

This strategy involves using trick questions or 'pressured selling' to encourage a buyer to choose a more expensive option and distract them from the standard option. You may choose a full-price magazine subscription, and then once that option is ticked, the site offers a subscription to the magazine's new online health site for an extra 'special offer' charge. 'Confirm-shaming' steers users away from declining by using prompts like 'Yes! I'd like this great offer' and 'No thanks, I don't want to feel healthier'.

Infinite scroll

Your search for a coat on a shopping site reveals that there are four pages of coats to view. That's doable, you think, so you start to scroll. However, as you get to the end of page four, more pages of coats magically appear. Now there are another four pages of coats to search! This can happen over and over again.

This dark pattern is designed to keep us scrolling until we're blue in the face, and we see this tactic on social media a lot. Think about those weird clickbait articles you often find on Facebook, where you go down a rabbit hole of endless links. Or Twitter's infinite scroll function, which makes you feel like there is always more to see. This fuels our dependency on technology by making us feel that there is always more.

Can't cancel

Have you ever tried to cancel an online account but you can't find the cancel option? It once took me several tries over a couple of weeks, and the help of a few friends, to cancel a rideshare account.

It might not be clear whether the account needs to be cancelled from within the app or if it must be done on the website, and you end up bamboozled by the many screens you have to jump through.

You may encounter many different forms of this tactic, but the goal of the developer is always the same – to frustrate you to the point that you give up and your account remains open.

Sneaky advertising

A friend's four-year-old son was playing a game online when an ad designed to look very much like the game popped up on the side of the screen. Thinking it was part of his game, he clicked on it, and it took him to a porn site.

Sneaky ads come in many forms and are disguised to look the same as the content on the page, tricking the user into interacting with the ad. This sometimes occurs in the form of a download button that tricks users into clicking other content instead of the real download. Product review sites can disguise ads to look like real customer reviews, even placing them in the same area as the actual reviews. Disguised ads are sometimes labelled as 'advertisement', yet even this label is often disguised, so it's easily missed.

Trigger-reward

You have likely seen the notifications that you get from games, shopping apps, emails or social platforms such as LinkedIn and Facebook: a pop-up message, or a little red dot or number on the app icon. In Silicon Valley terms, this is known as a 'trigger'.

Triggers are enticements used to keep us coming back. This dark pattern is a doozy, and it is a huge driver of the way we use our devices.

Facebook knows that a number three on their app icon will tap into your social cravings, and you will go into Facebook to see which three people liked your post. It's the same mechanism that keeps you compulsively watching a Netflix series, tapping into our innate compulsion to binge.

For smartphones, this trigger-action-reward system is particularly effective. It works like this:

1. You receive a notification (the trigger).

2. You then click on the app (the action).

3. You get an instant hit of dopamine as you see that someone has liked a photo or replied to a comment you posted (the reward).[57]

Social media sites like Facebook and Instagram work with several algorithms that determine your notifications or news feed. These formulas consider your previous interactions with others, as well as what you spend most of your time looking at on the site. However, these sites rely on a system called 'variable rewards'. This means that what pops up can *seem* quite random. A notification may be for a new video, a like on your photo, or a new follower: you won't know exactly what is going to show up, so you keep returning to check.

> The algorithms keep users guessing, and continually checking for more. They feed off our fear of missing out.

This stems from the work of psychologist BF Skinner, who predicted that creatures are more likely to seek out a reward if they're not sure how often it will be doled out. Pigeons, for example, were found to peck a button for food more frequently if the food was dispensed inconsistently, rather than reliably.

So it is with social media apps. Eighty per cent of Twitter posts may be a waste of time, but how many of us refresh our feed in anticipation of that elusive 20 per cent?

Our algorithm data is used to ensure that these triggers perfectly coincide with a time that you are mostly likely to interact with them. The time you see a notification often determines how you respond to it – whether it's late at night, during the working day, or when you are usually on the bus on your way to work. So, if you usually check your social media around 8 am, then these notifications will pop up just ahead of that time.

Sometimes notification algorithms will withhold 'likes' on your post to deliver them in larger bursts. This means that when you first upload your post, you may be disappointed to find fewer responses than you expected, only to receive them in a larger bunch later on. Dating apps do this, too. After a dry couple of days all of a sudden you will have five new love interests contact you.

As we are all distinct users, content and notifications are provided to us according to the individualised habits that we've formed. They are determined by our own specific algorithms.

What's an algorithm?

At almost every point during our day online, Google, Facebook, news outlets, online retailers and other companies you probably haven't even heard of track us online. If your device is turned on and has a signal, it can be communicating – whether you've asked it to or not. It's a bit like having thousands of peeping Toms looking over the fence, piecing together what we do across apps and websites throughout our day.

Companies use this information to join the dots about us, and categorise us in all sorts of ways. This is then used to predict our preferences and send that content our way.

Nearly all the content we might see on social media or in YouTube suggestions is chosen in this way. Not to mention the ads. You think it's a coincidence that yesterday you were googling Japan to plan your next holiday and today you're seeing ads about flights and tours to Japan? It's NO coincidence.

Organisations harvest platform data about us, crunching it to form demographic categories like 'Divorced, Male, No Children', and then selling this package to advertisers wanting to market their product.

You may also be classified according to your assumed financial situation – 'Urban Prosperity: World-Class Wealth', for example. This means that you have been deemed a global high-flyer or someone from a family of privilege living a luxurious lifestyle.

A business wanting to sell a new type of condom may purchase a 'Condom User Profile' from a Customer Profile Agency. This user profile may be determined by age, health, interests, occupation, family and home.

They then use this profile to determine who they target their ads to.

Obviously not all of this will be 100 per cent accurate, but the insight these companies have about us is fine-grained.

From your browsing history alone, it's possible to find out what work you do and what your interests are. They know your shoe size, that you have a penchant for gummy bears, and what kind of porn you like. Your credit card purchases indicate that you love bakeries. They know every movie you watch (including the ones you didn't finish) and which songs you skip or replay. Even your dreaming habits are monitored by sleep apps.

They dissect us and categorise us. That's how these companies make their money.

Personal data

Although there are benefits in receiving online content that fits with our interests, it's important that we strive for control over how commercial organisations treat us.

The ways companies persuade us to make choices online is becoming increasingly important, as more organisations turn to using personal data as a

While your feed, notifications, recommendations and advertising may feel random, it's all been carefully crafted by the algorithm to show whatever is most likely to keep us spending more or looking at their platforms for longer.

business model. Nowhere is that more evident than in the technology industry, where online platforms have built multibillion-dollar products out of the data that's generated when we click on ads or enter search terms.

Personally, I feel very uncomfortable knowing that political campaigns can buy data showing our personal habits and values, and use it for their own gain. One leaked example was the use of smartphone location data for people who had been inside Roman Catholic churches in a particular region to target political election ads. This tactic is known as 'geofencing', and there are many examples of it in the news – but perhaps not the news you read on social media, for obvious reasons.

Geofencing or 'ring-fencing', as it is also known, has become popular over the last several years, with advertisers, campaigns and advocacy groups using our geolocation data to find people who may be receptive to their message.

Ever wondered how much data is actually collected about us? An extraordinary investigation into the smartphone tracking industry undertaken by the *New York Times* showed that every minute of every day, dozens of largely unregulated and unknown companies log the movements of tens of millions of people and store this information in gigantic data files.[58] Each piece of data held the locations of a single smartphone over a period of several months. The data was collected by a location tracking company, using software slipped onto mobile phone apps.

Anyone with access to these data files can see whom we spend the night with or where we go – whether it's a methadone clinic, a massage parlour or a church.

All of this data is sent to organisations around the world, many of whom we've never heard of. How each piece of data will be used depends entirely on the organisation at the other end of the request. This has an unknown, and maybe even unknowable, effect on our privacy.

One journalist investigated how much data their phone and laptop sent and received in just one week. The journalist wasn't famous or being targeted for any reason – he was an ordinary person like you and me. And he found that his devices were contacted by another server 300,000 times, requesting information about him.[59] That's roughly one request every two seconds, and they even occurred when he was asleep.

Not all of the requests were sharing intimate private details about his life, but all of them, every single one, was sharing something about him. This might include updates for his email and calendar, or synchronisation of file-sharing apps. Some were from a travel app he had that seemed to be checking in every hour or so, presumably to see if he'd booked any new flights.

More information helps companies target their advertising, track high-traffic areas in stores or show us more dog videos to keep us on their sites for longer. For the companies, there's no downside to limitless data collection, and there's little to prevent this from occurring.

Undo the natural order

We're being tracked all the time. Internet superpowers hold enormous sway over what we see and what we buy. We've lost control over where our data winds up and how it's used. Our sensitive information keeps getting hacked. There's no simple fix for these complex worries. Unfortunately we've grown accustomed to the cryptic tactics organisations use to get our data. Constant trickery is disempowering. It wears us down.

French philosopher Jacques Rancière can help us here. He theorised about how people who are thought of as less than equal to others in society could gain equality – the poor, uneducated or powerless. In this case, we are the ones who can feel powerless against these huge technology companies.

Rancière suggested there is no reason why those on top should be in that position, and why those on the bottom should be there. That arrangement, he said, is due to the contingencies of history rather than the necessities of nature, and it is not something that we have to accept. The essence of equality, according to Rancière, is to undo the supposed natural order.

It can feel a bit like David versus Goliath when dealing with technology companies taking advantage of us. But knowledge is power.

Critically think about and examine the sites and apps that you use. Be more conscious of what you're doing online, what you've been falling for and what of yourself you're giving away. Ethical clothing and manufacturing processes are now valued more than ever. Ethical websites and apps should be given the same priority. Point your friends to these same ideas. Give them insight into the tricks being used on us. Something quite powerful can happen if we take action together.

Take action: use your data metrics for you

Our devices collect information about the way we use them. These digital metrics can show us how many times we pick up our device in a day or week, how much time we spend checking our email, using social media or searching Google.

This is valuable data not just for companies but for ourselves – it can help us understand ourselves as technology users and identify where we can make improvements.

A 15-year-old girl I was working with was shocked by the digital metrics on her phone, which showed that she had spent a full 24 hours that week on Instagram. It was a hefty dose of reality – she hadn't realised she was spending so much time scrolling Insta. She made changes in her use, and quickly got that number down.

Analysing trends regarding our online activity can be a powerful catalyst for making positive changes that will ultimately improve our health over time. If this data is being monitored, you can use it to your own advantage.

You can also limit what data is being collected about you. Every site you visit tracks the time you spend on there and leaves what are called 'cookies' on your device – you've probably seen notifications pop up asking you to accept them. 'Cookies' are like crumbs that keep track of everything you've done online. Companies use these to see what items you are browsing on shopping sites, what articles you're reading on news sites or what you are searching for on any given day.

When you clear your browsing history, the cookies are removed, and companies no longer have access to them. You can also take back control by browsing in private mode. Google calls this 'incognito mode', and Safari calls it 'private mode'. Doing this allows you to browse sites without cookies being collected.

Final word

Picture for a moment that you are swimming in the surf and get caught under a wave. The wave is quite powerful, and you find yourself getting tossed and turned. It's stressful until you break the surface and work out how to swim to shore.

For all the amazing opportunities technology offers, we have been stuck under the wave, drowning in notifications, misinformation, negativity and dark patterns.

But hopefully you now feel ready to take back control and swim to shore. What you accomplish over the next days, months and even years will be the direct result of what you do after closing this book.

A study by the University of Illinois found that the one thing that distinguishes the happiest 10 per cent of people is the strength of their social relationships. It makes sense, doesn't it? Have you noticed how often, when asked for a highlight of our day, we share a story about a great interaction with someone?

If your ultimate goal is to be happy, then use technology to learn and be more creative. But most of all, use it to foster a greater sense of belonging with family, friends, work and community groups, and to create more of those great interactions.

I have one last action point for you. Share this knowledge with others – your friends and family. Support them to make changes that will help them to be calmer, more in control and happier with, and as a result of, their technology uses. And remember, this is not a technology conversation, it is a life conversation.

References

1. Australian Bureau of Statistics, 2018, 'Household use of information technology', abs.gov.au/ AUSSTATS/abs@.nsf/allprimarymainfeatures/ ACC2D18CC958BC7BCA2568A9001393AE?opendocument.

2. Nielsen Digital Panel, December 2019, digitallandscape. nielsendashboards.com.au.

3. Global E-waste Monitor, 2020, itu.int/myitu/-/media/Publications/ 2020-Publications/Global-E-waste-Monitor-2020.pdf.

4. Oviedo-Trespalacios et. al., 2019, 'Problematic use of mobile phones in Australia … Is it getting worse?', Frontiers in Psychiatry, 12 March 2019, *frontiersin.org/articles/10.3389/fpsyt.2019.00105/full#B57*.

5. Shaw, V, 2020, 'Half of adults "take mobile phone to the toilet"', *Yahoo! finance, 12 February 2020*, uk.finance.yahoo.com/news/ half-adults-mobile-phone-toilet-000100802.html.

6. Winnick, M, 2016, 'Putting a finger on our phone obsession', *dscout*, 16 June 2016, blog.dscout.com/mobile-touches.

7. ibid.

8. Boyer-Davis, S, 2018, 'The relationship between technology stress and leadership style: An empirical investigation', *Journal of Business and Educational Leadership*, 8(1), 48–65, researchgate.net/ publication/328943900.

9. Oviedo-Trespalacios et. al., loc. cit..

10. ibid.

11. ibid.

12. Meagher, B, 2017, 'Problematic mobile phone use: An emerging disorder?', *InPsych*, October 2017, Issue 5, psychology.org.au/ for-members/publications/inpsych/2017/oct/Problematic-mobile-phone-use-An-emerging-disorder.

13. Marketwired, 2015, 'Landmark report: U.S. teens use an average of nine hours of media per day, tweens use six hours', *Yahoo! finance*, 3 November 2015, finance.yahoo.com/news/landmark-report-u-teens-average-050100412.html.

14. Ridley, J, 2018, 'One in 10 people checks their phone during sex: survey', *New York Post*, 7 June 2018, nypost.com/2018/06/07/one-in-10-people-checks-their-phone-during-sex-survey.

15. Morley, J, Widdicks, K, Hazas, M, 2018, 'Digitalisation, energy and data demand: The impact of internet traffic on overall and peak electricity consumption', *ScienceDirect*, sciencedirect.com/science/article/pii/S2214629618301051.

16. Auxier et. al., 2019, 'Americans and privacy: Concerned, confused and feeling lack of control over their personal information', Pew Research Center, 25 November 2019, pewresearch.org/internet/2019/11/15/americans-and-privacy-concerned-confused-and-feeling-lack-of-control-over-their-personal-information.

17. Pinoy, P, 2014, 'American Psychiatric Association makes it official: "Selfie" a mental disorder', *The Adobo Chronicles*, 31 March 2014, adobochronicles.com/2014/03/31/american-psychiatric-association-makes-it-official-selfie-a-mental-disorder.

18. Gardner, B, 2020, 'Three people treated for "binge watching" addiction to TV in first cases of their kind in Britain', *The Telegraph*, 6 January 2020, telegraph.co.uk/news/2020/01/06/binge-watching-tv-addicts-treated-harley-street-therapists-first.

19. O'Reilly, M, 2020, 'Social media and adolescent mental health: the good, the bad and the ugly', *Journal of Mental Health*, 29(2), tandfonline.com/doi/abs/10.1080/09638237.2020.1714007?journalCode=ijmh20.

20. Xue, B, 2009, 'A network ring center ecosystem (Electric shock therapy)', published online by Central Director of the Communist Youth League, Hosted by *China Youth Daily*, 7 May 2009.

21. Yan, A, 2017, '"No violence, electric shocks or drugs": new rules for China's internet boot camps for children', *South China Morning Post*, 9 January 2017, scmp.com/news/china/policies-politics/article/2060391/no-violence-electric-shocks-or-drugs-new-rules-chinas.

22. World Health Organization, 2018, 'Addictive behaviours: Gaming disorder', who.int/news-room/q-a-detail/addictive-behaviours-gaming-disorder.

23. UNICEF, 2017, 'The state of the world's children 2017: Children in a digital world', unicef.org/publications/files/SOWC_2017_ENG_WEB.pdf.

24. Stieger, S and Lewetz, D, 2018, 'A week without using social media: Results from an ecological momentary intervention study using smartphones', *Cyberpsychology, Behavior, and Social Networking*, 21(10), liebertpub.com/doi/pdf/10.1089/cyber.2018.0070.

25. Heyen, N, 2019, 'From self-tracking to self-expertise: The production of self-related knowledge by doing personal science', *Public Understanding of Science*, 29(2), 124–138, journals.sagepub.com/doi/full/10.1177/0963662519888757.

26. Nijssen, S, Schaap, G and Verheijen, GP, 2018, 'Has your smartphone replaced your brain? Construction and validation of the Extended Mind Questionnaire (XMQ)', *PLoS ONE*, 13(8), journals.plos.org/plosone/article?id=10.1371/journal.pone.0202188#pone.0202188.ref001.

27. Barr, N, Pennycook, G, Stolz, J and Fugelsang, J, 2015, 'The brain in your pocket: Evidence that smartphones are used to supplant thinking', *Computers in Human Behavior*, 48, 473–480.

28. Ottati, V, Price, E, Wilson, C and Sumaktoyo, N, 2015, 'When self-perceptions of expertise increase closed-minded cognition: The earned dogmatism effect', *Journal of Experimental Social Psychology*, 61, 131–138, doi.org/10.1016/j.jesp.2015.08.003.

29. Glance, D, 2015, 'Perhaps the only way to make money on a mobile app is to say you have brain cancer', *The Conversation*, 12 March 2015, theconversation.com/perhaps-the-only-way-to-make-money-on-a-mobile-app-is-to-say-you-have-brain-cancer-38679.

30. Spitzer, M, 2016, 'Outsourcing the mental? From knowledge-on-demand to Morbus Google', *Trends in Neuroscience and Education*, 5(1), 34–39.

31. White, RW and Horvitz, E, 2009, 'Cyberchondria: Studies of the escalation of medical concerns in Web search', ACM Trans. Inf. Syst. 27, 4, Article 23 (November 2009), 37.

32. Shiri, M, 2017, 'The distinct psychology of smartphone usage', Doctoral Thesis, Columbia University, academiccommons.columbia.edu/doi/10.7916/D8XH03HJ.

33. ibid.

34. Sup Park, C and Kaye, B, 2018, 'Smartphone and self-extension: Functionally, anthropomorphically, and ontologically extending self via the smartphone', *Mobile Media & Communication*, 2019, 7(2), 215–231, doi:10.1177/2050157918808327.

35. Asurion, 2019, 'Americans check their phones 96 times a day', press release, 21 November 2019, asurion.com/about/press-releases/americans-check-their-phones-96-times-a-day.

36. Wilson, et. al., 2014, 'Just think: The challenges of the disengaged mind', *Science*, 4 July 2014, 75–77, science.sciencemag.org/content/345/6192/75.

37. Hietajärvi et. al., 2018, 'Beyond screen time: Multidimensionality of socio-digital participation and relations to academic well-being in three educational phases', *Computers in Human Behavior*, 93, 13–24, www.sciencedirect.com/science/article/pii/S0747563218305843.

38. Tamlin, S, DeYoung, C and Silvia, P, 2016, 'Everyday creative activity as a path to flourishing', *The Journal of Positive Psychology*, 13(2), 181–189, tandfonline.com/doi/abs/10.1080/17439760.2016.1257049.

39. O'Dea, S, 2020, 'Number of smartphone users worldwide from 2016 to 2021', Statistica, statista.com/statistics/330695/number-of-smartphone-users-worldwide.

40. Gardner et. al., 2019, 'Physician stress and burnout: the impact of health information technology', *Journal of the American Medical Informatics Association*, 26(2), 106–114, academic.oup.com/jamia/article/26/2/106/5230918.

41. Arndt et. al., 2017, 'Tethered to the EHR: Primary care physician workload assessment using EHR event log data and time-motion observations', *The Annals of Family Medicine*, September 2017, 15(5), 419–426, www.annfammed.org/content/15/5/419.full.

42. Mark, G, Gudith, D and Klocke, U, 2008, 'The cost of interrupted work: More speed and stress', *Proceedings of the SIGCHI Conference on Human Factors in Computing Systems*, 107–110, www.ics.uci.edu/~gmark/chi08-mark.pdf.

43. Mobile Marketing, 2019, 'Why push notifications are only one part of mobile app win-back strategies', 30 April 2019, mobilemarketingmagazine.com/push-notifications-mobile-app-win-back-strategies-kumulos.

44. Royal Society for Public Health, 2017, 'Instagram ranked worst for young people's mental health', 19 May 2017, rsph.org.uk/about-us/news/instagram-ranked-worst-for-young-people-s-mental-health.html.

45. Salminen et. al., 2020, 'Topic-driven toxicity: Exploring the relationship between online toxicity and news topics', *PLOS ONE*, 15(2), journals.plos.org/plosone/article?id=10.1371/journal.pone.0228723.

46. Grubbs et. al., 2019, 'Moral grandstanding in public discourse: Status-seeking motives as a potential explanatory mechanism in predicting conflict', *PLOS ONE*, 14(1), journals.plos.org/plosone/article?id=10.1371/journal.pone.0223749.

47. Perez, S, 2020, 'Kids now spend nearly as much time watching TikTok as YouTube in US, UK and Spain', *Tech Crunch*, 5 June 2020, techcrunch.com/2020/06/04/kids-now-spend-nearly-as-much-time-watching-tiktok-as-youtube-in-u-s-u-k-and-spain.

48. Brady et. al., 2017, 'Emotion shapes the diffusion of moralized content in social networks', *Proceedings of the National Academy of Sciences*, June 2017, pnas.org/content/early/2017/06/20/1618923114.

49. Statistica, 2020, 'Online dating', statista.com/outlook/372/100/online-dating/worldwide#market-arpu.

50. Bruch, E and Newman, M, 2018, 'Aspirational pursuit of mates in online dating markets', *Science Advances*, 8 August 2018, 4(8), advances.sciencemag.org/content/4/8/eaap9815.

51. Kirley, E and McMahon, M, 2017, 'Emoji and the law: What happens when they're used to threaten or suggest violence?', *ABC News*, 5 December 2017, abc.net.au/news/2017-12-05/emoji-and-the-law-threatening-suggesting-violence-cases/9227136.

52. 'Making Sense with Sam Harris' podcast, episode 148: Jack Dorsey, 6 February 2019, podcastnotes.org/making-sense-with-sam-harris/Dorsey.

53. Stillman, J, 2019, 'Surprise: A new analysis of 777 million Facebook posts reveals positivity outperforms negativity', Inc.com, 14 January 2019, inc.com/jessica-stillman/the-3-types-of-content-that-do-best-on-facebook-according-to-a-new-study-of-777-million-posts.html.

54. Mathur et. al., 2019, 'Dark patterns at scale: Findings from a crawl of 11k shopping websites', *Proceedings of the ACM on Human-Computer Interaction*, November 2019, dl.acm.org/doi/abs/10.1145/3359183.

55. Harvard Magazine, 2011, 'HBS study finds positive yelp reviews boost business', harvardmagazine.com/2011/10/hbs-study-finds-positive-yelp-reviews-lead-to-increased-business.

56. Furchgott, R, 2020, 'How to spot fake reviews on travel websites', *Traveller*, 2 November 2020, traveller.com.au/how-to-spot-fake-reviews-on-travel-websites-h1rsgv.

57. Neuroscientifically Challenged, 2015, 'Know your brain: Reward system', neuroscientificallychallenged.com/blog/know-your-brain-reward-system.

58. Thompson, S and Warzel, C, 2019, 'Twelve million phones, one dataset, zero privacy', *The New York Times*, 19 December 2019, nytimes.com/interactive/2019/12/19/opinion/location-tracking-cell-phone.html.

59. Elvery, S, 2018, 'My devices are sending and receiving data every two seconds, sometimes even when I sleep', *ABC News*, 3 December 2018, abc.net.au/news/2018-11-16/datalife-i-spied-on-my-phone-and-here-is-what-i-found/10496450?nw=0.

Acknowledgements

There's a handful of very special people without whose help, commitment and enthusiasm this book would not be what it is. I want to start by saying thanks to Alana, Tom and Jack, you always believe in me and have supported me so amazingly in my work. I could honestly not have asked for more wonderful kids.

To my family and friends for their constant support and check-ins on the book's progress.

Thanks to my fantastic publishers at Hardie Grant Books, especially Emily, who provided insight and support during the production of this book. Thank you for trusting in my work and my instincts.

The biggest thanks to my agent, Jane, for all your guidance. Your insight was spot on.

Special thanks to my many research participants over the years, who have allowed me inside their worlds to understand how we truly think about our technology use. Without your generosity in sharing your innermost thoughts, I would not be able to do what I do. Also thank you to my esteemed fellow researchers, whose studies (including many I used in this book) provide an important basis for getting real and trusted information out about our relationship with technology.

This book has also been informed by the many people who follow my work and take up my solutions to the challenges that technology consistently throws our way. I feel privileged to have your trust, and to be able to make a difference in your lives.

Published in 2021 by Hardie Grant Books,
an imprint of Hardie Grant Publishing

Hardie Grant Books (Melbourne)
Building 1, 658 Church Street
Richmond, Victoria 3121

Hardie Grant Books (London)
5th & 6th Floors
52–54 Southwark Street
London SE1 1UN

hardiegrantbooks.com

A catalogue record for this
book is available from the
National Library of Australia

Life Mode On
ISBN 978 1 74379 705 1

10 9 8 7 6 5 4 3 2 1

Commissioning Editor: Emily Hart
Editor: Vanessa Lanaway
Designer: Mietta Yans
Typesetter: Hannah Schubert
Design Manager: Mietta Yans
Production Manager: Todd Rechner

Colour reproduction by
Splitting Image Colour Studio
Printed in China by
Leo Paper Products LTD.

MIX
Paper from
responsible sources
FSC® C020056

The paper this book is printed on is
from FSC®-certified forests and other
sources. FSC® promotes environmentally
responsible, socially beneficial and
economically viable management of the
world's forests.

Hardie Grant acknowledges the
Traditional Owners of the country
on which we work, the Wurundjeri
people of the Kulin nation and the
Gadigal people of the Eora nation, and
recognises their continuing connection
to the land, waters and culture. We
pay our respects to their Elders past,
present and emerging.